• HALSGROVE DISCOVER SERIES ➤

NORWICH

• HALSGROVE DISCOVER SERIES ➤

NORWICH

Stephen Browning

HALSGROVE

First published in Great Britain in 2009

British Library Cataloguing-in-Publication Data
A CIP record for this title is available from the British Library

ISBN 978 1 84114 854 0

HALSGROVE
Halsgrove House,
Ryelands Industrial Estate,
Bagley Road, Wellington, Somerset TA21 9PZ
Tel: 01823 653777   Fax: 01823 216796
email: sales@halsgrove.com

Part of the Halsgrove group of companies
Information on all Halsgrove titles is available at: www.halsgrove.com

Printed and bound by Grafiche Flaminia, Italy

Contents

NOTE

The author and publisher recommend the use of a city street map in conjunction with this book.
Maps are freely available from tourist information centres and there are also many commercially produced street maps.
Also currently available is a free guide and map for your mobile phone, see http://www.pocketnorwich.co.uk.

Introduction

'A Fine City'

Norwich is the most complete medieval city in Great Britain. It has, for much of its 1500 years been almost a separate kingdom – you don't go through Norwich to get to another important city or area – and this relative isolation has resulted in a mixture of architecture, character and customs that is unique. Almost every street has beautiful buildings wherever you look – up, down or straight ahead. There is an 'odd' balcony here, a beautiful gable there, and somewhere else an intricate footscraper or lovely doorway. If you are interested in old crafts, come see the original Town Hall with its squared flints or if you like to travel back in time, walk along Gentleman's Walk below the market where Regency Beaus used to parade up and down in their best finery.

Norwich has given birth or education to many eminent people – among them Baroness Amos, Philip Pullman, Admiral Nelson, Stephen Fry, Delia Smith, Kazuo Ishiguro, Ian McEwan, George Borrow and John Crome. Some famous industries have started here, too, including Coleman's Mustard, Caley's Chocolate, and Boulton & Paul who produced more Sopwith Camels in the First World War than anyone else. These, and many others, will be discussed in the walks around the town.

There is a new side to Norwich, too, best illustrated by the University of East Anglia, situated in 320 acres of lakes and woodland and originally built by Sir Denys Lasdun. This university, rapidly gaining in international distinction and number 2 in a survey of 'student satisfaction' in 2008 (only Cambridge did better) is fully open to the public and a separate chapter takes in the grounds.

There have been, in my opinion, some mistakes along the way. The Shopping Mall around the Castle is not completely successful and the Magdalen Street flyover has ripped the heart out of an ancient part of town. Some people slightingly refer to the new - 1938 – Town Hall as 'the marmalade factory' on account of the colour of the brickwork, but I think it is a fine, clean and elegant addition to the city and contrasts well with the 14th Century old Town Hall just below it. There is bound to be disagreement about some of the city's features but there is no doubt that, escaping as it did the ravages of the building 'boom' of the 70s, 80s and 90s, Norwich has largely retained its unique architectural character.

No book about Norwich would be complete without a chapter on churches. There are two inspiring Cathedrals and churches so grand, like St Peter Mancroft, opposite the Forum, that some visitors mistake them for the Anglican Cathedral. Then, there are churches that have been converted to other uses and some, sadly, that no one can work out an everyday use for. All, though, were the work of generations of families who laboured on them for the glory of God. They are quite exquisite and have many stories to tell.

Finally, this book ends with a walk around some of the many – though not so many as of old – pubs. In past centuries there were hundreds, many ordinary houses equipping their one and only day room with a barrel of dubious liquid to sell to neighbours. For many, leisure time was spent either building a church or drinking. Today, although the licensing trade is undergoing a hard time, there are still many fine pubs to visit around the city. Here, with a pint of Guinness, a glass of Chardonnay or whatever, you are invited to ponder the many wonders of this very special place. In the words of George Borrow, it is, indeed, 'a Fine City'.

Norwich Cathedral,
winter sunrise
(Daniel Tink - www.scenicnorfolk.co.uk)

River Wensum taken from Fye Bridge
(Daniel Tink - www.scenicnorfolk.co.uk)

Barrack Street

River Wensum

Cow Tower

Fye Bridge

Wensum Street

Cathedral

Bishopsgate

END

Riverside Walk

Riverside Road

Norwich Station

START

WALK I

Map not to scale
For general guidance only

Walk 1

A walk from the station along the river incorporating Pull's Ferry, Bishop's Bridge, Cow Tower, The Great Hospital, Mousehold Heath and a Riverside Walk

This walk begins at the station – there is only one now but there used to be three – as you get off an imaginary train from London pulling in to platform 2. The first thing to catch the eye is the Victorian wrought-iron pillars and intricate roof supports, now restored to their former glory in hues of lavender, white and powder blue. The concourse is large and bright as befits a major trading city. Stepping outside and looking back the view is more of an impressive country house, which was exactly what was intended by the eminent local builder, J. Young & Son, when he built the station in the years when Imperial pomp was at its height. It was formally opened in 1888: the year before had been Queen Victoria's Golden Jubilee.

Cross the street ahead of you and turn right past Foundry Bridge and you will find yourself on the banks of the River Wensum. Opposite is the colourful Compleat Angler pub.

Immediately below is Norwich Yacht Station. Looking up the river on a summer's day, many pleasure craft, small and large, can be seen moored on the river. Probably folk on board are tinkering about with the engine, sprucing up the paintwork or making tea.

The River Wensum itself meanders around the city and is part of the Norfolk Broads National Park, although not all of it is navigable to large craft. The area is home to a large and, at times, quite belligerent (if you get too close without bread or other edible redeeming features) community of swans.

A few hundred yards along and across the river is Pull's Ferry, marked by a 15th century water gate. The victorious Normans dug a canal here from the river in order to bring Caen stone from France as close to the cathedral as possible. Thereafter, the inlet was used to bring in provisions and, for at least 400 years, a ferry operated here. The keeper of the ferry was appointed by the Dean and Chapter and records show that in 1642 a man named Sandlin had the job: the ferry is presently known by the name of the last operator in the 1930s.

There used to be a pub beside the gatehouse. In late 18th century this and the surrounding riverside walk were notorious for drunken and immoral behaviour, so much so that one

The station – designed to impress

Foundry Bridge – an easily missed treasure as people rush to and from the city. Norwich has several beautiful metal bridges

Above left: A sunny summer's day will see plenty of activity on the river. This shot is taken by Foundry Bridge, just opposite the station

Above right: Boat trips can be taken from the Riverside Quarter

Pull's Ferry – once a disreputable part of Norwich

visitor called the area 'the roughest bit of picturesque Norwich'. After falling into disrepair the site was beautifully restored in the 1950s with money raised by Norwich Girl Guides.

Just past Pull's Ferry, the new visitor will gain an unforgettable first glimpse of Norwich Cathedral soaring above the playing fields of the famous Norwich School, where Nelson learnt his '3 Rs'. It is a view that has not basically changed for 900 years. In fact, almost everywhere you go in Norwich, the spire of the Anglican (for there is a Roman Catholic one, too, on the other side of town) Cathedral is there, above your left or right shoulder, a perpetual presence.

A few hundred yards farther along the river bank, on the left hand side, is a path leading down to the water. A gruesome find awaits, for alongside the path on the right is a large tablet set in the grass and easily missed. It commemorates the unfortunate souls who died in agony in Lollards Pit, the site of which is a little farther along, almost opposite Bishop's Bridge. A plaque on the Bridge House Pub commemorates the site. Many Christian martyrs, carrying their own bundles of firewood and preceded by chanting priests, were burnt at the stake here, in front of baying crowds. One spectator, Cicely Orme, went along just for the spectacle but was moved to pity by the sight of two dying men whom she comforted: for her trouble she, too, was tried and burnt at the stake.

One man who loved to walk around this area and up to Mousehold Heath was a favourite literary son of Norwich, George Borrow (1803-1881), who wrote *The Bible in Spain*, the novel *Lavengro* and much poetry besides. He was known in his youth as a lively chap who

Above: An unforgettable first glimpse for the visitor of the Anglican Cathedral. In the foreground are the playing fields of Norwich School

Right: Lollards Pit: everyone in the picture, apart from the poor souls being burnt alive, seems to be having a fine time. The scene is scarely worth a glance from the two gentlemen deep in convivial conversation to the right

The Burning of W. Seaman, T. Carman, & T. Hudson at Norwich.

liked to drink with his friends in and around Norwich. Later, he spent some time in Spain distributing bibles and preaching the Gospel. In *Lavengro* he describes a procession to Lollards Pit: 'many a grisly procession has advanced along that suburb, across the old bridge towards the Lollards Hole: furious priests in front, a calm pale martyr in the midst, a pitying multitude behind.'

Two sayings of George Borrow are particularly well-remembered. The first refers to his beloved Mousehold Heath where he would walk for hours: 'there's a wind on the heath, brother; if I could only feel that, I would gladly live for ever'. The other, his description of Norwich as a whole, has

become the city's slogan: 'Norwich, a Fine City'. It was replaced for a time by the much less catchy and rather arrogant 'Norwich: England's Other City' which has now been unceremoniously ditched.

A few yards down river to the north of the Lollard tablet, providing a pedestrian crossing point, is the beautiful Bishop's Bridge, so called because it led directly to the Bishop's Palace. This is one of the oldest bridges in the United Kingdom. We know it existed in 1249 as there are records of its repair by the See at that date. It is recorded that Elizabeth I travelled over the bridge to visit Mount Surrey, the palace of the Earl of Surrey situated on the top of what is now Gas Hill, behind you as you look towards the city.

The bridge had a narrow escape in 1923 when it was decided to 'widen' the roadway – this would have meant it would cease to be the only complete medieval bridge in Norwich. Luckily, in typically British fashion, it was left to a group of determined and stubborn citizens to oppose the idea. They were successful and the Norwich Society was born. The society has since fought many battles: won most, lost one (a big one sadly: the battle against the Magdalen Street Flyover, but more of that later) and is very influential today. It's headquarters are at the Assembly House, Theatre Street, or you can go to the website on www.thenorwichsociety.co.uk

Bishop's Bridge is etched in the Norwich mind alongside Kett's rebellion, the most bloody episode in the city's history. Following the Dissolution of the Monasteries, the lot of the peasant declined. Firstly, the monasteries had been, on the whole, a source of employment and benevolence: now they were gone. Then, the nobility and powerful landowners helped themselves to the common land of the peasantry by force. This was too much to take and in 1549 the common man found a leader in Robert Kett, a tanner from nearby Wymondham and a man of some education and high moral principles. He converted Mount Surrey on the

Kett is commemorated by this pub, close to where he made his last stand

hill overlooking Bishop's Bridge into a jail and threw the county's leading citizens, including the mayor, into it. 20,000 men rallied to his cause and camped out on Mousehold Heath overlooking the city. Kett petitioned the King and, by today's standards, his requests were eminently reasonable. The new King Edward VI, however, insecure on his throne and egged on by his advisors, chose to see the petition as a personal affront. He ostensibly offered a pardon to Kett and his followers if they would return to their homes and disarm. Kett rejected this with the famous words: 'kings are wont to pardon wicked men – not innocent and just men.'

An army was dispatched led by the Marquis of Northampton. Battle was joined and Kett won the day. Realising that he had underestimated Kett, the King then sent a much larger force under the command of the Earl of Warwick which breached the city walls and slaughtered many of the city's population. During the battering of the city walls, the top was lopped off Cow Tower to the extent that we see it today. Warwick took control of Bishop's Bridge, among other entrances to the city. Kett and his men tried in vain to cross the bridge into the city to reinforce his supporters. Wave after wave of brave men were repulsed and killed. Eventually, Kett retreated with the remnants of his army and made a last stand at Mousehold Heath. The result was slaughter.

Kett temporarily escaped but was captured in a nearby barn. He was hung over the side of Norwich Castle as an example to the people. Nine of his senior lieutenants were also hung from an oak tree called the 'Oak of Reformation', which was the tree under which, during the early years on the rebellion, Kett had received representations and issued orders. 45 more were hanged, drawn and quartered in Norwich Market Place. Another 250 were executed by various diverse means. It had cost the King the fantastic sum of £28 000 to put down a cause that most historians regard as just.

Ignoring the bridge for the moment, continue straight along the road to the roundabout. Turn right and walk past Kett's Tavern. Swing around to the back of the pub and you will see a footpath leading up to Mousehold Heath. There is a fine view of both Cathedrals, the Castle and Town Hall from the top. If you wish, you can walk for miles on the heath, most of which is behind you as you look down upon the city. For this walk, though, make your way back again to Bishop's Bridge.

Crossing Bishop's Bridge, carry on straight for a few hundred yards and look to the right. Here is The Great Hospital, founded in 1249 by Walter de Suffield, Bishop of Norwich. The hospital was originally home to a Master and 4 priests, 4 elderly sisters – classified as over fifty years old – all chaplains in the diocese who were 'decrepit' and 13 other sundry poor persons. Wholesome school dinners were also to be provided for 7 children in need. Good to relate, the Great Hospital carries on its work today and is one of the most beautiful and peaceful places in Norwich.

Some of the accommodation provided by the Great Hospital

The approach to the Great Hospital

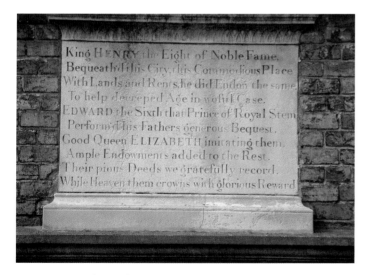

King HENRY the Eight of Noble Fame,
Bequeath'd this City, this Commodious Place
With Lands and Rents, he did Endow the same,
To help decreped Age in woful Case.
EDWARD the Sixth that Prince of Royal Stem,
Perform'd his Fathers generous Bequest.
Good Queen ELIZABETH imitating them,
Ample Endowments added to the Rest.
Their pious Deeds we gratefully record,
While Heaven them crowns with glorious Reward

Henry VIII and Elizabeth I played their part in funding the Great Hospital and, according to this stone tablet, will reap 'glorious reward' in heaven

The riverbank by Cow Tower is a mass of daffodils in Spring

Cow Tower – the top was shot off by the Earl of Warwick. Once a toll house, it was later a grim prison

The inside of Cow Tower, showing the thickness of the walls

Detail of Cow Tower. Precision archery would have been needed to steer an arrow through this gap

A modern block complements this elegant mill which once held 600 looms

Doubling back down the road, turn left at the Red Lion and through an alleyway which leads to the riverbank. In the Spring and early Summer, the banks in this area is resplendent with many varieties of wild daffodils.

Straight ahead is the 12th century Cow Tower. It was originally a toll house where monks would take a fee from merchants who wanted to proceed upstream. Later it became what must have been a very grim prison before ownership finally transferred to the City at the end of the 14th century. This part of the walk, with many benches facing the river and in peaceful spots a little inland, is ideal for a rest or picnic. It is completely quiet today but it is not hard to imagine the bustle of monks and ships amid the cries of the unfortunates in the tower.

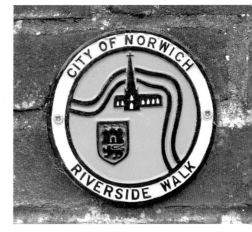

In case you get lost, there are always plaques to guide you on your way

Carry on walking along the river and you will see on your left, beyond a small car park, the Adam and Eve Pub, reputedly the oldest in Norwich and featured later in the pub walk. A few hundred yards farther on, to the right on the other side of the river, is St James' Mill, built in the late 1830s. It is a handsome ivy-covered structure, more like some strange, exotic hotel than a weaving factory. At its peak, there were two steam engines which powered over 600 looms, all let out to different people. Many others set up a manual loom at home. Unfortunately, Norwich could not compete with Yorkshire and by 1900 the textile industry had all but vanished. St James' Mill later became a printing works.

You have to cross the busy road ahead before again walking down to the river. This part of the waterfront has recently been restored with great success. New houses are mixed in with the refurbished originals, some brick and others painted in attractive traditional colours – a deep rose magenta, light blue, and cream, and the streets have been paved with flint. Along the bank you will see a series of sculptures which, at first sight look like heavy slabs of wood bounded by rusting iron bands. Closer inspection reveals that each 'bale' is engraved with the name of one of the commodities, businesses or people associated with quayside life over the past 200 years. So we have 'Thomas Fielding', 'Noverre Shoes Ltd', 'Anglian Wholesalers' and a 'Mrs Peck'. They are stacked, higgledy-piggledy, against each other.

Modern sculptures, each of which is inscribed with a person, trade or activity associated with the river

Ahead you will see Fye Bridge. It was here that, until the practice ceased in 1587, 'harlots' and 'scolds' were ducked using the cucking stool. This was a particularly fetid part of the river and one duck was a light punishment and three a heavy one. As with burning at the stake and hangings, duckings were the centrepiece of a family day out, complete with music, dancing and eating.

Turn left at Fye Bridge and a couple of hundred yards brings you to the Maids Head Hotel on your left. A hotel for over 700 years, it has many secrets. A distinguished former mayor of 1611, Thomas Anguish, is commemorated by the ancient 'Anguish doorway' on the corner as you are just coming up to Tombland. He apparently spent more time here than he did at home, as have many others since. 'The Courtyard' restaurant is a good place to have a meal or afternoon tea.

You are now in Tombland – nothing to do with tombs, but deriving from 'thum', meaning 'empty' space. This walk ends here. If you want to get back to the starting point carry straight on until the crossroads with Prince of Wales Road and turn left where a downward walk of ten minutes leads past the kebab shops and nightclubs back to Foundry Bridge. Much more beautiful, however, is to cut through the Cathedral Close via the Erpingham Gate on the left where a short stroll will take you to Pull's Ferry. Turn right here and proceed past the boats, swans and weeping willows that bow so low they touch the water, to Foundry Bridge.

This doorway celebrates Thomas Anguish who spent more time at the Maids Head than he did at home. His wife was not best pleased

A good place for a meal, afternoon tea or a drink – the Courtyard at the Maids Head Hotel

Norwich skyline - featuring from left to right: Norwich Castle, St Peter Mancroft, the Forum, City Hall, Norwich Cathedral and St John the Baptist Cathedral
(Daniel Tink - www.scenicnorfolk.co.uk)

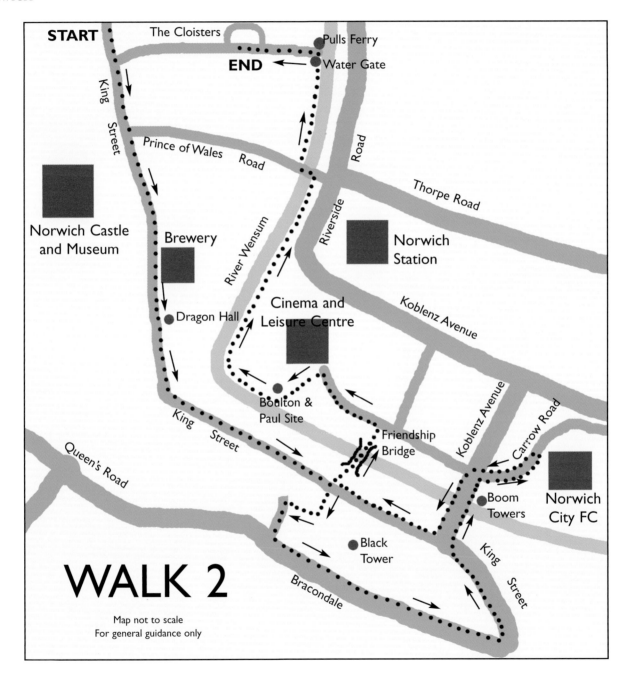

START

The Cloisters

Pulls Ferry

END → Water Gate

King Street

Prince of Wales Road

Road

Thorpe Road

Norwich Castle and Museum

Brewery

River Wensum

Riverside

Norwich Station

Koblenz Avenue

Dragon Hall

Cinema and Leisure Centre

Koblenz Avenue

Carrow Road

Boulton & Paul Site

Friendship Bridge

King Street

Queen's Road

Boom Towers

Norwich City FC

Black Tower

King Street

WALK 2

Bracondale

Map not to scale
For general guidance only

Walk 2

A walk through Tombland, along King Street, up to Bracondale, down to the Norwich Football Ground (the team is nicknamed 'Canaries') and Riverside Quarter, ending up in the Cathedral Close

This walk is a hefty one and needs a good half day and probably something relaxing – the pub section of this book may help – afterwards.

Tombland was the original market place of Norwich and today is a mixture of fine restaurants, solicitors' offices, buses and cars. Watch you don't get run over. On your left you will see the Erpingham Gate, built in 1420 by Sir Thomas Erpingham who commanded the victorious archers at the Battle of Agincourt. Look up and you will notice a stone statue of him in prayer, thanking God for having spared his life.

The monument to Edith Cavell in Tombland: her grave is alongside the cathedral

Adjacent to the gate is a memorial by Henry Pegram to one of Norwich's great heroines – Edith Cavell. A nurse in Belgium in 1914, she set up an escape organization for wounded soldiers and managed to help over 200 to safety. She was subsequently arrested, tried entirely in German which she did not speak, and shot in 1915. On the night before her death, she made the famous remark that 'Patriotism is not enough' as she would willingly have helped soldiers of any country. Her body was brought back after the war and now lies in a peaceful spot in the Cathedral Close. Almost opposite the memorial is a pub named after her.

Tombland was the scene of a riot in 1766 over the high price of corn - shops of bakers and millers were sacked. Two people were hanged in 1767 as a consequence.

Walking up to a busy intersection you will see ahead of you perhaps the grandest Post Office in the Kingdom. It was the Crown Bank originally but the bank went bankrupt. Now it is being converted into flats. To your right is the Royal Hotel, designed by Edward Boardman, which gives the unsettling impression of rather too much having been crammed into the sky. It is beautiful, with some lovely mini turrets adorning the top, and exquisite brickwork, but it does not seem able to breathe. Perhaps the space on which it is built is simply too small. It is now given over to a variety of offices.

Solicitors' offices and Spanish restaurant in Tombland

Proceed straight ahead into King Street. This was one of the first areas of Norwich to be inhabited, and extremely important it was too. Rich merchants, the Howards – Catherine

Edward Boardman's Royal Hotel

Lovingly preserved dwellings in King Street – once by far the most important street in the city

Medieval detail on King Street

Dutch gables in King Street, bearing testimony to the influx of refugees

was Henry VIII's fifth wife – and the Dukes of Norfolk all had houses here. John Caius, physician to Edward VI and founder of the college at Cambridge that bears his name, was born here. The main industry was beer making and the most famous firm was Morgan's: sadly, one of the founders, Walter Morgan, was overcome by the powerful yeast fumes in a vat of beer, fell in and drowned.

About five minutes' walk down King Street, on the left hand side, is Dragon Hall, a magnificent merchant hall belonging to Robert Toppes, four times mayor of the city. Grade I listed, it dates from 1420 although the site has been occupied since around the time of the Battle of Hastings in 1066. It is well worth a visit. There is a fee payable but this is reduced for family groups.

Down the street a few yards is what is reputed to be the oldest occupied house in Norwich – the Music House. This fine building, where we know the Jurnet family lived, bears testimony to the wealth of the Jews in Norwich in the 11th and 12th centuries. It is possible that the first ever recorded case of prejudice against the Jewish people flared up at about this time. What happened was as follows. The Jews probably came to the UK with William the Conqueror. By their skill and hard work, and especially by the granting of loans – some say that the cathedral itself would not have been built without this 'liquidity' facility – the community of about 200 Jews became very successful. Unfortunately, they also aroused envy. In 1144 the mutilated body of a 12 year old boy was found on Mousehold Heath and

Above left: The magnificent Dragon Hall in King Street

Above right: Probably the oldest private dwelling in the city – the Music House

the story spread that he had been tortured and murdered by the Jews in a mock crucifixion. Miracles were claimed to be occurring at the place where he was buried. Resentment thereafter bubbled under the surface of society. We will never know the whole truth. What we do know is that in 1275 Edward I forbade Jews to loan money with interest and that in 1290 they were thrown out of the country altogether.

Almost next door is Wensum Lodge, which is the centre for adult education in Norwich. Hundreds of courses are available, from art to Russian and from piano tuition to yoga: details at www.norfolk.gov.uk/adulteducation.

Proceed down the street, past the Novi Sad bridge, popularly known as the Friendship Bridge, on the left, a white and striking affair, until you come to Southgate Lane on the right-hand side. This is not a lane at all really but a fairly narrow and steep set of steps and pathway leading up to Bracondale. Turn left at the top and enjoy a leisurely descent along a most elegant wide road with some fine houses. Many people prefer this area to the more famous 'Golden Triangle' on the other side of the city. It has always been noted for the number and quality of its schools. Bracondale School was one such and had a famous pupil

Left: Entrance to Dragon Hall

Right: The dragon above Dragon Hall – is it me or does it look like a demented bee about to sting you?

in Bill Edrich who was selected for the Norfolk cricket team as a teenager and subsequently broke many records when playing for England.

At the base of the hill, you will meet King Street again on your left. About five minutes walk as you proceed, turn right into Carrow Road and across the river. You will see the ruined remains of Boom Towers on the riverbank where once heavy metal chains strung between the towers prevented any unwanted ships passing upstream into the city.

This is the location of the factory of perhaps Norwich's most famous export – mustard. The Colman family established a huge business refining the famous yellow paste, later branching out into starch, laundry blue and other products. What is most remarkable, however, is that they set standards of care for the workforce that were unheard of in early 18th century England. There was a male and a female medical team; a school was set up for children of workers and Mrs Jeremiah Coleman herself used to cook the employees a lunch of stew, bread and coffee all for 4 pence (that's old 'd'). Very popular, too, were the day trips for the whole workforce. Trowse, just a little farther out, was a model town – it is still there – on the lines of Bourneville, providing clean and sanitary accommodation for all workers. Jeremiah was a just patriarch, and much loved. When he died in 1898, 1200 workers from his factory followed his cortege. The company now belongs to a multi-national corporation but the Colman's Shop, in the Royal Arcade, is a popular tourist spot and mustard will forever be associated with Norwich.

Left: A fine stretch of the old city wall at the top of Bracondale

Right: Attractive housing in Bracondale

Bracondale is a desirable residential area.

Details of oak beams in front of the Dragon House

As young boys growing up in the healthy air of Hunstanton, my brother and I had bottomless stomachs and one way my mother used to cope with this was to sometimes give us what we called 'Mum's Mustard Mash'. The great thing about it is that the cost is low, it is extremely healthy and quite delicious. It can be used to complement almost any dish from bacon and eggs to a full roast, and also makes an unusual crisp and golden topping for shepherd's, chicken or vegetable pie when baked in the oven for about half an hour. Mum used to make it using Colman's original powdered mustard, which I still think cannot be beaten for taste: however, it is less work and fine to use the ready-made type. Here is the recipe.

Mum's Mustard Mash
Ingredients
4 or 5 medium to large potatoes, peeled and quartered
3 or 4 chopped cabbage leaves
2 carrots, peeled and chopped
1 tablespoon Colman's Mustard – original recommended but any variety can be used
Small amount of milk and butter
Salt and fresh ground pepper

Method
Boil potatoes for about twenty minutes until tender. Separately, boil carrots until cooked – about 15 minutes – adding chopped cabbage with about five minutes to go. Mash potatoes, using a small amount of milk and a knob of butter. Add all ingredients together and add the mustard, salt and pepper. Serve immediately to hungry boys and girls of all ages. Alternatively, it can be kept in the fridge and served as part of a full English breakfast next morning.

Straight ahead, you cannot miss the Canaries Football Ground. Originally called the Citizens, the present name took hold early in the 1900s and derives from the fact that Norwich was a centre for canary breeding, the birds themselves having come over with Dutch settlers in the 1500s. Every Saturday when playing at home, fans in bright green and yellow strip flood in from all over Norfolk. The glory days were in 2004 when the Canaries made it to the very top and spent a giddy year in the Premiership. Even the staid Town Hall went a little mad and perched a massive yellow inflatable canary on the roof

Thousands of loyal fans flood through these gates every time 'The Canaries' play at home

The Novi Sad or 'Friendship Bridge' leads from one of the oldest parts of the city, King Street, to the most modern. New flats, on the left and a retail park can be seen here

Modern flats by the football ground

overlooking the Market. Sadly, they could not avoid relegation at the end of the first season and in 2009 were further relegated, but the fans are still fervent.

A Director of the club and known as 'The First Lady of Norwich' is the legendary cook and food writer, Delia Smith. Is there anybody who does not have one of her books? Certainly not around here. She has established a restaurant in the ground itself. She is brave, too. She has been known to stand in the ground with a microphone and demand more support from the fans when things are not going so well. Another famous fan is Stephen Fry, actor, author and TV presenter, who spent much of his youth in the city and attended Norwich City College.

Cut back to the river from the Football Ground and take in the view from halfway across the Friendship Bridge, or Novi Sad Bridge as it is officially called. Norwich is twinned with four overseas cities – Novi Sad in Serbia, Rouen in France, Koblenz in Germany and El Viejo in Nicaragua. The idea of twinning is a positive outcome of the last World War, the aim being to increase understanding and friendship between different people. Norfolk and Norwich Novi Sad Association is particularly active. For more information contact twinning@norwich.gov.uk

This is new Norwich, looking across the Riverside Quarter towards the Anglican Cathedral. There is a selection of one, two and three bedroom luxury flats and duplexes as well as pubs, nightclubs, restaurants and a cinema complex.

A fine flying machine, manufactured by Boulton & Paul, on display at the 1919 Paris Air Show

You are also looking at the site of Boulton & Paul, a famous firm that began in Rose Lane and moved to larger premises by the river in the 1920s. Initially doing reasonably well manufacturing just about anything in metal, their big break came when a machine for the mass production of wire netting was perfected. This coincided with a huge order for netting from Australia which was having difficulty controlling rabbits. Thereafter, the firm diversified into aircraft production and produced more of the famous Sopwith Camel aircraft during the First World War than anyone else. They were tested out on Mousehold Heath. The block of new flats immediately in front of you is named after another of their aircraft, the 'Sidestrand' bomber. Just by the bridge you will also find two unusual and starkly beautiful memorials to Boulton & Paul created in cast iron and copper. The firm has subsequently relocated to Wolverhampton.

From the river bank you can walk along the river towards the Cathedral Spire in the distance. Half way along, you will come to 'The Queen of Iceni' and 'Norwegian Blue' pubs, discussed further in chapter 11. This is also the setting for a variety of restaurants and a multiplex cinema. The river is also home to many varieties of duck as well as the ubiquitous white swan.

You are now almost back at the station. If you have the energy – if not a bus from the station will carry you quickly up to the Castle – cross Foundry Bridge, walk through the outside area of the Compleat Angler pub where people are drinking and along the river. When you come to Pull's Ferry, turn left up through the Cathedral Close and take a seat at the top opposite the new herb garden. You will not fail to notice that, to your left, is a fine statue of one of Norwich's most famous adopted sons, His Grace the Duke of Wellington, victor of Waterloo, who is looking out past his fine aquiline nose to check that you are behaving yourself.

This walks ends, and the next one starts, here.

Details of one of two sculptures celebrating Boulton & Paul, just below the Friendship Bridge

Modern luxury apartments in the Riverside Quarter: Norwich has not gone 'overboard' in the provision of modern apartments

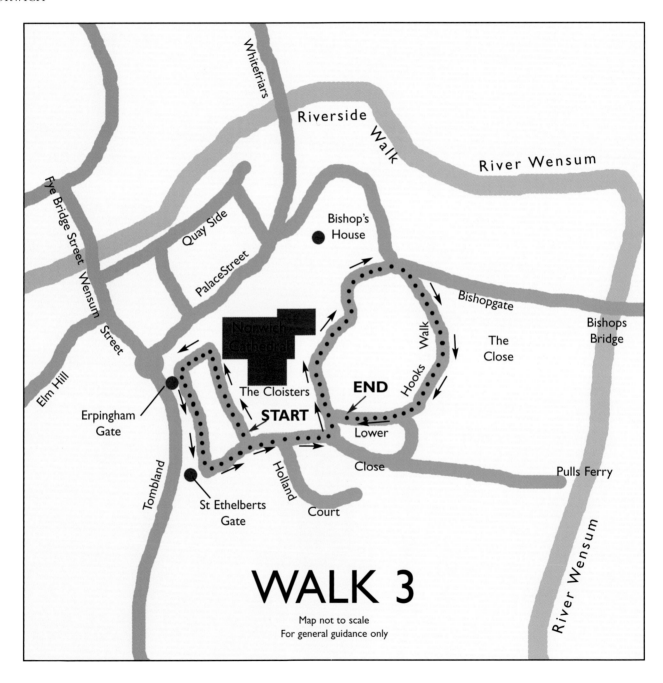

Whitefriars

Riverside Walk

River Wensum

Quay Side

Palace Street

Fye Bridge Street

Wensum Street

Bishop's House

Norwich Cathedral

Bishopgate

Bishops Bridge

The Close

Elm Hill

Erpingham Gate

The Cloisters

Hooks Walk

START

END

Lower

Tombland

St Ethelberts Gate

Holland

Court

Close

Pulls Ferry

River Wensum

WALK 3

Map not to scale
For general guidance only

Walk 3

Around the Cathedral, Cloisters and Close

A friend of mine who is now an eminent professor at a university in Asia was, some years ago, considering whether to go to the USA or UK to do his doctorate. It so happened that the British Council put on an exhibition about Britain in his home town and it contained a picture of Norwich Cathedral. There was something about the building that intrigued him and he subsequently spent four happy years at the University of East Anglia, since when he has returned regularly. Numerous contacts have resulted. There must have been many untold stories like this over the centuries.

Before touring the Cathedral proper, it is well worthwhile to take a walk around the building and to explore the Upper and Lower Close. Some of the houses are quite lovely, some very grand indeed, while others are of more modest dimensions.

In the Cathedral Close are lovely houses from many different architectural periods

Norwich Cathedral

Quirky and handsome (above): details of architecture in the Cathedral Close

Cathedral Close (above): with the detail of a new building imaginatively complementing one much older
(Daniel Tink - www.scenicnorfolk.co.uk)

Some of the architectural styles which sit neatly together in the Close

Traditional English country gardens front some of the houses

Strangely, the Cathedral probably started life as an act of penance. Herbert de Losinga became notorious when he paid King William II a huge sum of money for himself to be made Bishop of Thetford and his father Abbot at Winchester. He went to Rome to seek absolution and moved the centre of his See from Thetford to Norwich in accordance with the wishes of the Pope - important cathedrals should be in large towns. Work started in 1096. This story is depicted in the earliest paintings in the Cathedral.

The building progressed rapidly as Herbert de Losinga was an enthusiastic and hard taskmaster. When he died in 1116, the most important part – the eastern end where the altar is – had been completed. The rest followed shortly afterwards. Misfortune necessitated rebuilding work: the first spire was destroyed in the great riot of 1272, the second blew down in a storm in 1362 and the third was felled by lightning in 1463. The present one, the second highest in England, is actually made of brick with a thin veneer of stone and is, one hopes, safer.

The Cathedral is open every day from 7.30 am to 6.00 pm – slightly later in summer. If you would like to go to a service, there are five each weekday at 7.30 am, 8.00 am, 11.00 am, 12.30 pm and 5.15 pm, the middle three being Holy Communion. Taking pictures is allowed although you are asked to 'buy' a photo permit at the main door.

Flint cottages in the Close

Norwich Cathedral Cloisters
(Daniel Tink - www.scenicnorfolk.co.uk)

The newly planted herb garden: the walk passes by on the way into the Cathedral

A good way to start the tour is by the side entrance, alongside the herb garden. On the right-hand side before this entrance lie the remains of the priory infirmary. There were sixty or seventy Benedictine monks here and they lived an austere and poor life. They rose just after midnight in summer and had a single meal twelve hours later. In the cloisters you will see their book cupboards and also washing facilities. It must have been cold in winter. As you look around at the stone pillars and window arches that grace the four sides of the cloisters, you will notice that, clockwise, the stone tracery becomes more complex. Experts will tell you that this is because the masons became more skilled as the work progressed.

One reason for spending some time in the Cloisters is that one of the glories of the Cathedral is the roof bosses and here, as opposed to in the Cathedral itself, they can be seen clearly just above your head. They are fabulous and tell complex tales: for example, one tells the story of Salome dancing seductively, demanding the head of John the Baptist as a reward, the beheading of John, and the presentation of the severed head to her – all in a small roof boss. Then there are biblical scenes, morality tales, domestic tales, many mythical creatures, lots of devils, while everything seems to spring out of golden foliage, the significance of which which still perplexes historians. There is humour, too: one you will see depicts a furious row between a husband and wife, and it has been suggested that the purpose of this was to show the monks that marriage was overrated. Here, and inside the Cathedral, the kingdom of heaven bears an uncanny resemblance to Norwich Castle which, of course, was the grandest thing that any of the master stonemasons would have seen.

There is a fun maze on the grass quad. Good use is made of this area by local schools.

Before leaving the cloisters, it should be said that there is a new, very pleasant but perhaps a little pricey café which has been cleverly built on the side. There are toilets, too, on the ground floor.

Finally, before entering the Cathedral proper, you may want to take a look at the Cathedral library which is on the first floor beside the café. There is a lift. It is a small, bright room with, as you would expect, a collection of about 25,000 religious works. However, it also contains some books on poetry, architecture, medicine, local history and music. You can sit, read or work in an oasis of peace, but it is not open every day, so best to check in advance. If you wish to take books out, this is fine but will cost, currently, £12 a year.

You enter the Cathedral at the bottom left of the Cloisters (looking at it from the angle you came in). This is the south transept and, continuing into the nave aisle, stop to consider the famous skeleton memorial to Thomas Gooding and, particularly, its message about mortality. Turn right, and you will soon come to St Luke's Chapel. Gaze behind the altar to view a priceless work of medieval art – the Despenser Reredos. Apparently, this only survived the destruction of the Reformation because someone had the idea of turning it on its back and using it as an everyday workman's table.

Below left: Detail of archway leading into Cathedral

Below right: Detail of a roof boss in the Cloisters

Detail of artwork on the walls of the Cloisters

Detail of roof boss in the Cloisters

Roof boss – one of many restored to original glory

Ancient graffiti on the stone seats in the Cloisters

Nearby are the votive candles, where you can say a prayer if you wish and light your own candle.

Straight ahead, looking down the Cathedral, step into the Presbytery where the tomb of Herbert de Losinga will be found. Behind the High Altar is the 'cathedra' which means 'teaching seat' and it is this which gives the church the status of a Cathedral.

As you proceed down the Choir, look up at the bosses which we have already talked about. There is an ingenious mirror table to help save your neck muscles. There are over 1000 in here and they tell the tale of human life from Adam and Eve to Doomsday. Unlike those in the cloisters, these have a key architectural purpose, being 'keystones' which lock the roof vaults together. Because of this, they were inserted as plain pieces of stone and carved by the masons in situ.

Walk ahead into the Choir. The seats here are from the 15th Century and are carved with all sorts of scenes, some of them very funny and tell their own story.

The altar is ahead of you and is where Holy Communion is taken.

Lockers in the Cloisters: monks would keep their books here

A 19th century view of the Cathedral showing a Wherry transporting goods along the river: this was how the Caen stone used in the construction was brought to the Cathedral

Looking from the presbytery to the east window: the Bishop's Throne can be seen at the far end and it is this which bestows upon the church the status of a cathedral

The unique font in the cathedral was once used for making chocolate

The amazing main window straight ahead is one of the most photographed in England. The rich stained glass dates from the 15th Century. Many other glass panels are even older and a separate walk around the Cathedral rewards the visitor with the sight of stained glass which not only contains dates and uplifting sayings but hues of, say, amber, blue and red that are not reproduced today.

You will not fail to notice a large copper bowl as you walk on. This is the font, but was previously a vat for producing chocolate at Caley's factory, a famous Norwich enterprise.

Before leaving by the West Door, you may want to visit the shop to your left or chat to the staff at the reception desk to your right. As you would expect, there are expert guides – look out for a green sash – who will gladly take you around again and have many tales to tell of the history of this place.

Look back, as you leave the West Door, at the statues of St Benedict (480–527) and Mother Julian (1342–1416). They were designed by David Holgate and erected in 2000 to mark the 900th anniversary of the Cathedral's foundation. Julian is holding her book *Revelations of Divine Love*, discussed in Walk 10, while St Benedict is bidding the visitor to be silent on entering this holy place.

Above left: Exquisite 16th century stained glass in the Cathedral

Above right: Details of window: note the varied and subtle shades of colour used

41

Julian of Norwich greets visitors above the West Entrance

St Benedict bids you hush and remember God as you enter the West Door

Outside the West Door is a statue of, arguably, Norwich's most celebrated son, Admiral Lord Nelson, who attended Norwich School for a period. He is claimed by many cities, notably Portsmouth, but he is reported to have said 'I am a Norwich man'. This statue, of Sicilian marble, was erected in 1874 and cost 700 guineas. Nelson's victories were numerous, most famously at Trafalgar in 1805, where he defeated the combined French and Spanish fleets by a daring manouevre which attacked the opposing convoys in the centre. This isolated them from each other and he was able to 'pick them off' one by one. As everyone knows, he was killed in the battle. This was probably because he did not have the time to change his clothes. Resplendent in medals, he must have looked like a Christmas tree and was picked off by a marksman on a French ship. His victory, together with that of the Duke of Wellington ten years later at Waterloo, secured the domination of Britain in the the 19th century world by both land and sea. The British Empire had no opposition. Both of these British heroes have statues on this green.

Looking out from the West Door through the Erpingham Gate towards Augustine Steward House

You are now at the Erpingham Gate. Stroll left across the grass, past the schoolrooms used by Norwich School. Maybe, if the weather is fine, there are lessons being conducted on the grass. In a weekday, there will certainly be many blue blazers around. To your left is the other gate to the Cathedral, the Ethelbert Gate. Turn left and you will find yourself at the starting point of this walk. You may wish to sit down on the same bench whence this tour started.

The next tour will take in some rich history but in some more down-to-earth parts of town.

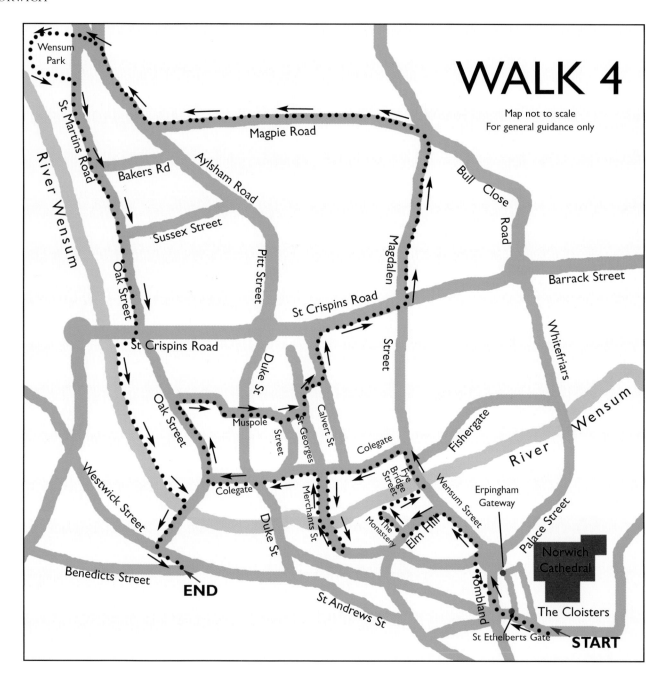

WALK 4

Map not to scale
For general guidance only

Wensum Park

St Martins Road

Bakers Rd

Aylsham Road

River Wensum

Sussex Street

Oak Street

Magpie Road

Pitt Street

Bull Close Road

Magdalen Street

Barrack Street

St Crispins Road

St Crispins Road

Whitefriars

Duke St

Oak Street

Muspole Street

Calvert St

St Georges Street

Colegate

Fishergate

River Wensum

Westwick Street

Colegate

Merchants St

Fye Bridge Street

Wensum Street

Erpingham Gateway

Palace Street

The Monastery

Elm Hill

Norwich Cathedral

Benedicts Street

Duke St

Tombland

The Cloisters

END

St Andrews St

St Ethelberts Gate

START

Walk 4

A walk from Tombland, taking in Elm Hill, Colegate, Coslany, Magdalen Street, Wensum Park, and parts of the River Wensum

This walk begins on the spot that the last one ended. Walking slightly uphill, you will see once again the statue of the Duke of Wellington on your right. The Duke had no direct connection to the city, although his son served as MP for Norwich. The 19th century was an age of putting up statues – this one, made of bronze, was erected in 1854.

Pass through the Ethelbert Gate and pause to look back at the top of the archway where there is a fine medieval depiction of a battle between St George and the Dragon. Turn right into Tombland and stroll along the cobblestones noting the array of upmarket cafés and restaurants, past the Edith Cavell pub on your left and the memorial to her on your right, and cross the road at the pedestrian crossing. To your right you will see a heavily timbered house with not a right angle or straight beam to be seen. This is Augustine Steward House, built in 1549 and headquarters of both royal armies who quelled Robert Kett's rebellion in that year. Augustine Steward was Mayor of Norwich three times – in 1534, 1546 and 1556. In 1924 the house was bought and restored by the Norfolk Archeological Trust. Pass through the alleyway to the left of the building for a good look at the side and details of the oak beams. The house is now used as an antique market .

Many parts of Norwich are associated with the Black Death, including this area, where numerous bodies are supposedly buried. The plague wiped out two-fifths of the citizens – the

His Grace, the Duke of Wellington, occupies a beautiful spot in the Cathedral Close. He did not have any direct connection with the city but his son served as Member of Parliament

Morning coffee in Tombland

Autumn colour in Tombland

Tombland Alley, one of many peaceful oases to be found unexpectedly in the city

Hardly a straight line in sight: the incomparable Augustine Steward House

Detail of ancient timberwork on Augustine Steward House

Elm Hill: saved from destruction by just one vote

total population of the city was 18,000 at the time – when it struck in 1349, 1361 and 1369. The plague was carried by rats which thrived in the unsanitary conditions of the period. Nobody really understood this then, however, and all sorts of theories were espoused as to the cause, from germs spread by damp and fetid air, to the revenge of an angry God. The monks were particularly badly hit as it was they who tended the sick. Paradoxically, a good thing to come out of all the death and disease was a shift in the balance of power between the working man and the nobility as well as other employers. As there were simply very few people left alive to tend the fields, build houses and so on, wages shot up. The worker could almost state his own terms and his former subjugation was gone forever.

Coming out of Tombland Alley and walking toward the Maids Head Hotel, you pass on your left some smart new flats with a most unusual doorway. Over-lifesize statues of Samson and Hercules guard the entrance to what was once Samson and Hercules House. Formerly a nightclub, it is reputed to be haunted.

Fine dining is available in Tombland

Just past the Maids Head Hotel, on the left is one of the most famous streets in the city - Elm Hill. Apart from the Anglican Cathedral, this must be the most photographed place in Norwich. It is so named because there used to be two huge Elm trees at the top which have, sadly, succumbed to disease. The walk winds up this cobbled street, past the many small shops selling prints and antiques. On the right you will see an alley down to the quayside whence boat trips can be taken. Elm Hill has undergone several distinct changes. In the thirteenth century it was a centre for monks (Friars de Sacco and later the Black Friars). In the fifteenth century it had become a very fashionable part of town and notable inhabitants included the Paston family. The *Paston Letters* is a classic of English social history, reflecting the complex relationships between influential families in England during the troubled period 1422-1509: it is still in print today. During the Victorian era the street fell into disrepute and decay. It is reported in council records that early in the 20th century it was saved from demolition and redevelopment by just one vote. Half way up you will see, to your right, the famous Strangers' Club – 'Strangers' simply means people from outside the UK – where fine wining and dining have been the norm for centuries. The original building did, however, burn down in 1507, killing several people. Now, some locals will not pass by late at night because it is claimed that frantic footsteps can sometimes be heard.

Princes Street looking towards the church of St George, Tombland. You can dine in an Italian, Japanese or English restaurant here

Elm Hill – cobbled streets and perfectly proportioned timber-framed buildings

Elm Hill: note the gabled top stories which would have produced enough natural light to allow inhabitants to make shoes or weave cloth

By the river just off Elm Hill – planning regulations were once much laxer!

Don't go past at night... (see text)

Elm Hill: a visual delight

The Briton Arms: note the fine thatched roof

Elm Hill was selected to become a bustling street in the 2007 film hit 'Stardust' starring Robert de Niro, Michelle Pfeiffer and Sir Ian McKellen.

At the top of the street is the Britons' Arms, with its fine thatched roof, dating from the reign of Elizabeth I. Turn right here and walk down to and along the river towards Fye Bridge. This is a lovely spot, perfect for a picnic or a quiet read. You will come up to the main road again alongside the Ribs of Beef pub.

Turn left, past The Ribs of Beef pub, over Fye Bridge, past The Mischief pub and turn into Colegate immediately past the Church of St Clement. Notice the fine black and gold clock. The inscription reads 'Restored in memory of the Fallen 1939–45'.

Elm Hill: many small specialist shops thrive here

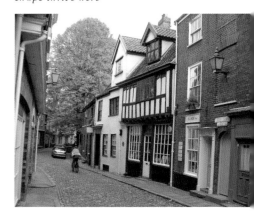

Colegate is my favourite street in Norwich as, if one street can encapsulate the spirit of a city, it is this one. Some of the city's finest church architecture, meeting houses, industrial buildings, pubs and fine old houses all vie for attention. There are many architectural details too – an intricate footscraper here, an elaborate pillar top there, lead plaques commemorating the date of construction and initials of the builder on some other buildings along with informative plaques to Amelia Opie, authoress and reformer, and various famous sons and daughters of Norwich.

River Wensum and Fye Bridge
(Daniel Tink - www.scenicnorfolk.co.uk)

Walk past the flint walls of the remains of the town house of the Priors of Ixworth, and later home to John Aldrich, MP and Mayor in 1558 and 1570. It is now offices. You will see an alley to your right which leads to the Old Meeting House, dating from 1643. If the sun is out, you can check your watch on the elegant sundial facing you. The Meeting House is still in use today for a variety of functions. Retrace the few yards back to the main road.

Here are some superb examples of three storey houses where the top floor served as a workshop, primarily for shoe production. There are many fine top storeys all over Norwich, the area determining what trade used to be carried out. You will find some in other parts that have seemingly over-large windows to the third floor: these were for private looms where light was essential in the production of cloth.

On your right is the famous Octagon Chapel designed and built by Thomas Ivory in 1756. John Wesley was said to be so struck by it that he was afraid that people would spend their time looking around at the beauty of it rather than listening to his preaching. It is discussed further in Walk 10. This was also the site of the Conventual Church of the Norwich Black Friars in 1226.

Fye Bridge Street – one of the shortest streets in the land

Sarah Glover
1786-1867

Originator of the Tonic sol-fa notation with her sisters Christina and Margaret founded a school for gentlewomen in Black Boys Yard

Far left: View from the top of Colegate looking towards Coslany

Left: This plaque, just off Colegate and easily missed, bears witness to the importance of the area in women's education

*Operating a hand loom: many
people, such as 86 year old
James Churchyard, pictured here,
relied on weaving for a living.
This picture was taken
in 1913*

Across the street is the Merchants of Colegate Pub - previously The Black Boys. It is worth a slight detour here up Merchants Street, recently beautified and repaved by the City Council. Passing some fashionable restaurants on both sides of the road, you come to a paved square and grass area bordering the river. To your right is Norwich Playhouse, the centre for live performances in the city: comedians, one man shows about cricket, Greek tragedies, live bands – they all come here as you can see from the colourful chalkboard display by the main entrance. There is a café/bar with an outside seating area bordering the river that is popular with all ages.

When you come to Blackfriars Bridge, designed by Sir John Sloane in 1784, notice the stark but grand Norwich Technical Institute, built in 1899, on your left. Turn back and retrace your steps to Colegate.

At the crossroads your eye will be caught by the heavily timbered pink building opposite. This was the house of Henry Bacon who was Mayor in 1548, 1557 and 1566 and whose intitials can be seen on a stone tablet inserted into the wall.

On your left as you walk is what was once the headquarters of Norvic Shoes. A friend of mine from overseas found it hard to believe that a factory could be so elegant. But this was, until 1980, the very epitome of modern shoe production and employed assembly line techniques more often used in car production. It is a grand building, designed to make a statement. Now it is mostly offices.

Opposite is St George Colegate, now restored after the partial collapse of the tower in 2007. This is where John Crome worshipped and, inside, is a fine memorial to him. He was the most eminent of the so-called Norwich School of Artists which flourished in the early 19th century. Born in a pub in Tombland in 1768, Crome began his career as a painter of coaches and tavern signs. As his reputation grew, he was able to take

The Merchants of Colegate, now a restaurant and bar, previously called the Black Boys

Middle: Norwich Playhouse: a vibrant centre for the arts and a very pleasant drinking establishment which is popular with all ages

Above right: Want to know what's coming up? This colourful chalk board outside the Playhouse will tell you

Plaque commemorating another historic metal bridge just past the Playhouse: the walk doubles back from here

advantage of the patronage of local gentry such as the Gurneys of Earlham. Most of his works are of Norfolk. He is now regarded as one of the three great English landscape painters of the century, along with Turner and Constable. He married in 1792 and had eleven children, some of whom also became artists of note.

Colegate continues across Duke Street ahead of you. Here you will see St Michaels of Coslany. It is now used as a children's hands-on museum and is a good example of imaginative use of empty church space, of which the city has rather a lot.

Turning right, you are looking down Oak Street, probably the first part of Norwich to be inhabited. This area is called Coslany, which may mean 'island with reeds' or, again, it has been suggested that it may mean something like 'area of the pigmen', presumably not a compliment. Just beyond the smart houses to your left is the River Wensum and it is along the river that the first ribbon of dwellings developed in Saxon times. Later, the centre of town moved to Tombland and this area declined rapidly. In the late 19th century it was the centre of the cloth dyeing industry – note 'Indigo Yard' to your left which commemorates the trade – and was the scene of terrible poverty. 'Yards' where, city records show, as many as 10 or 15 people shared one house, led off from the street to the water. A typical Norwich Yard consisted of a number of two-roomed dwellings at one end of which would be a communal washroom, cooking facilities and toilet. As late as 1925 records show that the council wanted to pull down 3000 houses in this area as they were not fit for human habitation. The river was used for all purposes: for dyeing cloth, drinking, making beer and for the disposal of human and other waste.

Top: The house of Henry Bacon, thrice Mayor of the city

Middle: The mark of Henry Bacon

Bottom: Surely this is too elegant to be a factory? The old Norvic shoe plant in Colegate, now offices

Once the scene of great poverty with 'yards' running down to the river, Coslany has recently been redeveloped. The houses generally have living rooms on the first floor to take advantage of the view

New housing alongside older in St Miles Alley

Walk on a little and turn right into St Mary's Plain. Ahead you will see the round tower of St Mary's Church. This style is popular in Denmark and Sweden, so there is speculation that there were once communities from those countries in the area. Luke Hansard was baptized here in 1752 and went on to found Hansard, surviving to this day as the official record of proceedings in the House of Commons in London. Fittingly, the church is currently used by a printing firm.

Cross the road into Muspole Street, cut through a small alley called Alms Lane on your left and proceed into Cross Lane. Here you will see a plaque to John Crome who lived nearby. Around here somewhere was The Rifleman pub in which John Crome reputedly spent many evenings.

The Church of St Mary: the round tower is typical of Denmark and Sweden. Probably communities from those countries settled here

As you come to the end of the street, the Magdalen Street flyover is straight ahead. There is a walking path to the side which leads to Magdalen Street. This, one of the most historic areas of the city, was also the scene of controversy when the flyover and adjacent Anglia Square shopping centre were built in 1970. As you come to Magdalen Street and turn left you will see some beautiful and quirky eaves and houses as well as an interesting mix of shops and cafés but the area as a whole has a down-at-heel feel which many people attribute directly to the modern developments. When Anglia Square – to your left as you walk – was first built, it did, indeed, look as if the area was going to be revitalized as some large companies rented offices here but, at the time of writing, the future of the area is unclear.

A famous resident was John Gurney who established his banking firm in Gurney Court: this later became Barclays Bank. Elizabeth Fry (1780-1845), the famous prison reformer and Quaker, was born here.

Magdalen Street: the area is rich in intricate architectural detail, often above eye level

Magdalen Street: you could be in Sicily

Turn left down Magpie Road, follow it to the bottom and turn right into Aylesham Road. After a few minutes, cut left through Drayton Road and ahead of you is one of Norwich's best-kept secrets: Wensum Park. This is a quiet park with a small wood at the farthest end. There is also an enclosed childrens' play area . The river runs alongside and it is sometimes possible to see nesting swans as well as a large variety of ducks. There are toilets here.

Leaving the park, proceed back to the city along St Martin's Road which leads into Oak Street. Further evidence can be seen here of Norwich 'Yards' leading down to the river. You cannot get lost here as you will see Norwich Town Hall clock towering ahead, beckoning you on.

Turn right at the main road, cross it and, ignoring Oak Street, go a little further along where you will see a strange boarded-up structure, a little like an octagonal tardis, on the banks of the river. This is one of the first urinals in the city. Note the state-of-the-art ventilated roof.

Passing by, you are now strolling along the banks of the River Wensum, parallel to Oak Street, where the numerous slum Yards used to lead to the water. It is a very different picture today, with a clean river and a modern development of balconied houses and flats extending along it on both sides. Halfway up you will pass the gently slushing New Mills Sluice, restored in recent years by a charitable trust.

Rejoining Oak Street and turning right over St Miles Bridge, dating from 1804, the eye is caught by a large brick-coloured building on the side of which, in gold letters, is written 'Bullard & Sons' Anchor Brewery'. This is a clue to the other main activity in this area for many years – brewing. The building has now been imaginatively turned into flats. Ahead is the huge structure of St Laurence Church, perched in a most unlikely position on the side of a hill. To the left, the walk leads up steep steps known as St Lawrence Steps – the spelling is indeed different from that of the church – to St Benedicts Street, where this walk ends and the next begins. This is an excellent street to find a café for a snack or full meal and has several old pubs, too. If you want to get to the centre of the city, just follow the flow of people through the jumble of Norwich Lanes: it is only a few minutes away, straight ahead of you as you come up the steps on to St Benedicts Street.

Nesting swan in Wensum Park

A Victorian Tardis? No, a very early men's urinal: note the state-of-the-art ventilated roof

Another fine metal structure of which the city has many – St Miles' Bridge dating from 1804

Anchor Brewery, Coslany

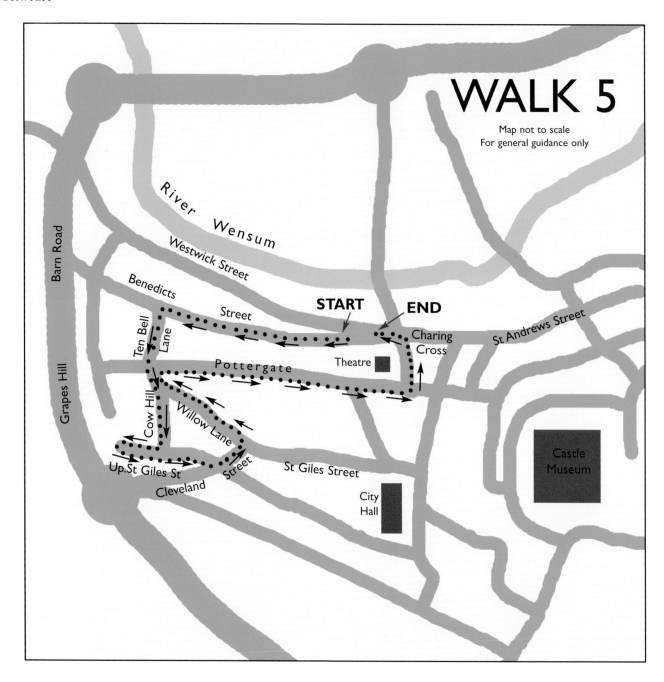

WALK 5

Map not to scale
For general guidance only

Walk 5

A walk through St Benedicts Street, Cow Hill, Upper St Giles Street,
Pottergate and the Lanes, taking in Maddermarket Theatre and Strangers' Hall

Starting from the top of St Lawrence Steps and turning right, a slow stroll down St Benedicts Street will reveal four churches and an eclectic array of shops and cafés. Here you can buy a trombone, a wedding dress, a rare book, an easel and paints, a focaccia sandwich, a craftsman-made pine chest, some gem stones to bring peace to your house, a T-shirt that, for some reason says 'POW-ZAT!', tinned vegetables from Poland, a scale model of Goldfinger's Rolls Royce, a house plant from Peru, and a pair of skis for your next visit to St Moritz. You can buy French, Greek, Italian, or Indian food as well as English pub grub. You can convert your unwanted presents and household items into cash. You can chill out in a sports bar with a giant plasma screen or linger over a pint of Guinness in a traditional pub such as the Ten Bells. And all of this is within a few hundred yards of the starting point.

St Lawrence Church: the railings after a fresh fall of snow

Notice the Norwich Arts Centre on your right as you walk down the street. Here, again, is an imaginative use of an old church. There is live music, interactive exhibitions, storytelling, poetry nights, live music, photographic courses and all sorts of things taking place in the Centre. It also contains a peaceful café.

A welcome sight for hungry walkers

St Benedicts Street Annual Fair

Almost opposite the Arts Centre, turn left into Ten Bell Lane where the walk starts to get quite steep. On the corner with Pottergate, you will pass the Micawber Tavern, named after the famous character in Dickens' *David Copperfield* who always believed that 'something will turn up'. Walk straight ahead and along Cow Hill towards the imposing church of St Giles on the Hill. At the top of the hill turn right into Upper St Giles Street. This is a pretty street where you can dine in some first class restaurants – advance booking recommended. It also houses some of the city's most notable delicatessens and patisseries where everything from home-made organic scotch eggs to take-away crème brulees are available. You will pass some shops selling reclaimed architectural features and antiques, so here is the place to come for a Victorian marble fire surround or an original oil painting from the Regency period.

Upper St Giles Street is notable for speciality foods and is also the place to come for architectural antiques and curiosities

The street comes to a sudden end as the Grapes Hill dual carriageway cuts rudely across it. A fine view of the Roman Catholic Cathedral is in front of you (covered in a separate walk). For now, cross the street and start to walk back along Upper Giles Street.

At the top of the road is a plaque commemorating that fine English actor, Sir John Mills, who went to school here. Apparently, he hated it. Sir John provides another link to Charles Dickens in the public mind because one of his most celebrated roles was Pip in 'Great Expectations'.

Charles Dickens loved Norfolk. Some of his greatest writing features the county – notably Great Yarmouth which stars in *David Copperfield*, Dickens' favourite of all his novels. In *The Pickwick Papers*, Mr Pickwick and Sam Weller, the characters that propelled him to international fame at the age of 25, also had some memorable adventures in Norfolk. Famously, the hilarious description of an election at Eatanswill in the book is a critical but affectionate comment on Norwich. Dickens writes that '…the Eatanswill people considered

Far left: Commemorative plaque

Left: Upper St Giles Street with the Roman Catholic Cathedral in the background

The fine clock on the Church of St Giles on the Hill

themselves of the utmost and most mighty importance…'. Both political candidates hilariously go out of their way to flatter the citizens, calling them independent, noble, public spirited and disinterested. It is also documented that Dickens came here to witness one of the last public hangings and that he was appalled at what he saw. Thereafter, he campaigned against this barbaric practice, particularly the 'party atmosphere' of the proceedings. He was a hero in his own lifetime and is credited with helping to change the people's attitude to public punishments.

Walk back down the street and past the impressive Church of St Giles on the Hill, the gardens of which, in Spring and Summer are a riot of colour in a classic English way with giant specimens of hollyhocks and foxgloves almost hiding the lower parts of the church walls. A wonderful lilac wisteria winds around the wall beside the road. Turn sharp left down Willow Lane: just where it meets Cow Hill, on your right, is a plaque commemorating George Borrow – discussed in Walk 1 – who lived here.

Far left: George Borrow pops up all over the city. This plaque is in Cow Hill where he lived for a while

Left: The gardens of the Church of St Giles on the Hill are a delight in summer

Pottergate
(Daniel Tink - www.scenicnorfolk.co.uk)

The locally famous wisteria of the Church of St Giles on the Hill

Turn right into Pottergate. This ancient street has been the centre of many trades. The name derives from the pottery industry that existed prior to the 13th century. Shoe manufacturing peaked in the 18th and 19th centuries. An eye infirmary established here eventually became incorporated with the Norfolk and Norwich Hospital. The famous, and much loved opera singer, Jenny Lind established a Hospital for Sick Children here in mid-Victorian times. More recently, it became the home of Norwich Job Centre and some English Language Schools – a modern-day Norwich industry. George Borrow pops up all over the city and here is no exception as he lived in Pottergate for a period.

One of the Norwich Lanes – Goat Lane – in the 1930s

Ahead is St Gregory's Alley. A pleasant grass area with refurbished seating, it is an oasis for many folk who sit down, on the grass, new seating or low walls in front of St Gregory's Pottergate, to have a bite. There is a delicatessen, a fish and chip shop, some sandwich bars and a juice bar all within a few yards. St Gregory's Pottergate is now a craft centre with a café and The Birdcage pub borders the green. You are now at the very centre of Norwich Lanes and perhaps you would like to browse around the Lanes to the north, south, east and west of this spot, and continue the walk when you get back. Many compare this to the more famous 'Brighton Lanes'. The many small entrepreneurs who trade around here are the perfect antidote to 'samey' high streets throughout the country – you will see traders in exquisite evening dresses, antiquarian booksellers, an Egyptian pottery merchant, some 'New Age' herbalists, an expert in military clothing, a trader in the latest computer games, a Fair Trade enterprise, someone selling tea from all over the world and teapots of fantastic designs, and many more. It is constantly changing as you would not expect, sadly, every new bright idea to survive. Norwich has always been thus, however – as one trade goes down, another comes up. For this to happen, there has to be a crucible of creativity. Here it is, at least as far as retail goes, for the modern age.

*St Gregory's Alley – always a
popular spot for a rest or snack*

Street entertainers in the Lanes

Commemorative plaque

You will, I am sure, note the recently refurbished street furniture and the attractive green and gold square plaques inserted into the walkways which tell tales of life and businesses in days gone by.

There are three more important stops on this walk. Unfortunately, one of them, The Bridewell in Bridewell Alley is not available for visitors late 2008–2011 as it is closed for refurbishment. It tells the story of Norwich industry – mustard, textiles, chocolate and beer. The building itself is a sombre flint edifice and it is not hard to believe that it was once a prison for beggars – 'bridewells' – and women. If you go around the building to the opposite side you will find the original small oak doorway, blackened and cracked with age, through which prisoners passed to begin their sentence.

Commemorative plaque

Street furniture

Street plaque

Carry on a few yards until you come to St John's Alley which runs down the side of a fine small church, St John Maddermarket, which houses the finest collection of brasses in the city. The name 'Maddermarket' is derived from 'madder, which is a Norfolk plant that produces a red dye. Half way down, you will come across The Maddermarket Theatre. This is special because it welcomes local people to act and help out in putting on professional productions. There is also a plaque commemorating the feat of the most famous Morris dancer of all time, Will Kemp. In 1599, for a bet, he Morris danced ('lustily', according to his tomb in London) all the way from London to Norwich. It took him four weeks and he ended his journey, to great acclaim, in this alley where he jumped over the graveyard wall of St John Maddermarket opposite the theatre entrance. He was given a pension of 40 shillings a year.

At the bottom of this alley is an ancient water pump that served the needs of the area.

Somewhere in this vicinity during the reign of Elizabeth I was the Palace of the Duke of Norfolk, and we know from the letters of guests that is was a malodorous place, being too close to the river as described in walk number 4. Reputedly, he plotted here to marry Mary, Queen of Scots, and lost his head as a consequence.

At Charing Cross, turn left and a few more steps will find you at Strangers' Hall. This is a gem. The building itself dates from 1320 and contains imaginative recreations of life in Tudor and Stuart times. In the Great Hall, the high table is set for a feast which gives an inkling of the excessive carbohydrate diet enjoyed (endured?) by wealthy merchants prior to modern-day notions of healthy eating. The 17th century bedroom of Lady Paine (wife of Mayor, Sir Joseph Paine) is open to public view. There is a collection of historic toys, too. A costumed guide will show you around. It is open 10.30–4.30 Wednesday and Saturday. A charge is made for entry. As with most Norwich museums, a disabled visitor is able to bring along an able-bodied friend for free.

This walk ends here – you are a few yards from where it began.

Strangers' Hall – an absolute 'must-see'

Below left: Maddermarket Theatre: notable for welcoming local citizens to act, and help out, in performances

Below: Ancient street pump and modern seating in Charing Cross. The wall shows the depth of the 'raised' burial ground of the church of St John Maddermarket

Walk 6

A walk from Bethel Hospital, taking in the Theatre Royal, Assembly House, Surrey House, Timberhill, the Castle and the Royal Norfolk Regimental Museum

Mary Chapman was born in 1647 and, after her husband died, dedicated her life to the foundation of a hospital for the 'curable lunaticks' of Norwich. The Bethel Hospital cost over £300 to build and in 1728 had 28 patients, most of whom received care for free. This was remarkable for its time – existing mental hospitals were private and very expensive. The Bethel Hospital continued well into the 20th century. It is now converted into apartments and marks the start of this walk, opposite the Fire Station in St Giles Street. If you walk around it's walls you will find yourself in Theatre Street and, on the opposite side of the road is the Theatre Royal resplendent after a multi-million pound refit

The original theatre dates from 1758 and it was designed by James Ivory. It was very small and a new Theatre Royal was built in 1826 which attracted the famous actor, Edmund Kean, who played King Lear in 1830. Some contemporaries considered the plays staged here to be superior to anything that London had to offer. Close by, roughly on the site of the Millennium Library, was the White Swan public house which was (in)famous for more popular types of musical entertainment, as well as being a centre for cock-fighting. Another well known drinking establishment was the nearby Rampant Horse which, in 1785, boasted a 'learned pig' able, so legend has it, to answer questions by selecting letters and numbers set out in front of it: apparently, he grew more remarkable as inebriation increased.

Far left: The Theatre Royal, resplendent after a multi-million pound refit

Left: The original entrance to Bethel Hospital for 'curable lunaticks', remarkable in its time for being mainly free

The road train will take you around the inner city and can be caught from Theatre Street

Below left: Game of lawn chess anyone? The front of the beautifully understated Assembly House

Below right: Looking out from the Assembly House towards the BBC Centre in the Forum

Opposite the Theatre Royal is the spot to wait for a tour, either by bus or 'road train'. The former currently goes quite far afield and the latter just takes in the city centre. Either is a good way to gain a sense of perspective as regards the city and is especially welcome when the legs begin to tire.

Nikolaus Pevsner, the famous architectural historian, was greatly impressed with the Assembly House which you will find a few yards from the Theatre Royal, on the right as you look – literally – down the street. Built on the site of the College of St Mary, which was founded in 1248, the present house, of pleasing symmetry, dates from 1754 and was designed by Sir Thomas Ivory. As you approach, you may see, in summer months, a huge chess set on the lawn and, at all times a little nearer the main entrance, a beautiful bronze statue of a boy with a waterlily bud, crafted by James Woodford and erected in 1954.

The Assembly House was designed as a centre of entertainment for the gentry and its dances, recitals, displays – Madame Tussaud came here in 1825, and Franz List in 1840 – and victory celebrations of the Imperial period were very popular and successful. Unfortunately, its fortunes declined thereafter, and it was used for many things – a dance academy, a cinema and as an army office during the Second World War. It was restored in 1995 but, tragically, an electrical fire swept through it almost immediately causing damage that would have been irreparable but for the foresight of one man, forty years earlier: Mr Barratt, a trustee during the war, had commissioned details of the marble, gilding, carving etc to be photographed precisely in case of such an eventuality. These were used during reconstruction: thus we can be sure that the building we see today is authentic in every way.

Proceed downhill to the crossroads and, on your left, is Debenhams department store, previously Curl Brothers. In one of the doorways you will see, on the floor, a mosaic of a rampant horse. This was the site of the Rampant Horse public house, referred to earlier which took its name from the Horsemarket which was held in this street. It was also from here that you might catch the coach to London – the other main coaching depot was at the Maids Head Hotel. A great scandal arose in Victorian times when it came to light that coaches from the Rampant Horse illegally transported, unbeknown to fare-paying passengers, crated corpses to London for sale to the various medical schools. If you died in the workhouse – and Norwich had at least two very large ones – you would very likely suffer this fate. It was more than a dreadful indignity as people believed that only those who had all their bones buried with them would be able to enter the Kingdom of Heaven: hence the terror of some figures depicted by Charles Dickens and other contemporary novelists at the thought of dying in a workhouse. In *Our Mutual Friend*, Dickens depicts a man who, having had his leg amputated, goes to great lengths to buy back the sawn-off part so that it can be placed alongside him in his tomb.

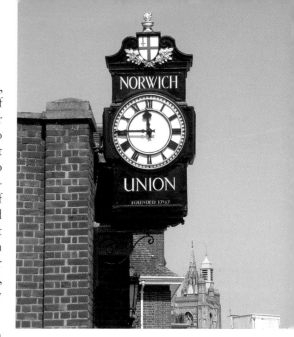

Turn right here and then first left. This is Surrey Street, and, a little up on the left-hand side is one of the most remarkable buildings in the East of England – Surrey House. It is also the headquarters of Norwich Union, now part of Aviva Worldwide. Designed by George Skipper, it looks far older than it is – it was, in fact, opened in 1904. The true wonder, however, begins inside as you step into the magnificent main hall which is fully open to the public. The style is English Renaissance and the forty columns as well as stairs, door architraves, window pilasters and ornate carvings are made from 15 different types of Italian and Greek marble. Here we have Cipollino, Verde Antico, Skyros Rosso, Rosso Antico, Pavanazzo, Belgian Blue and Sienna marble, to name just some. The story goes that the marble was originally ordered for the Palace of Westminster but, not being able to afford this particular shipment, the Palace sold it to George Skipper for the knockdown price of £6,000. The building has many wonders, including a 'world first' air conditioning system which works via a marble fountain in the centre of the hall, and some 16th century stained glass. The building was designed, like the Bank of England in London, to impress upon visitors the solidity and affluence of the company and it certainly succeeds. You may wish to linger here a while and it is fine to take pictures.

Top: The most famous clock in the world apart from Big Ben? The spires of the City Hall and Victorian 'enhanced' St Peter Mancroft can be seen in the distance

Middle: The marble interior of Aviva Worldwide – a team of Italian craftsmen were brought over to execute George Skipper's designs

Bottom: Wyverns on the outside of a remarkable building belonging to Aviva Worldwide, previously Norwich Union

Walking up Surrey Street, you pass the new state-of-the-art Bus Station on your right. Note the revolutionary curved roof which saves heat. Turn left into All Saints Green and sweeping ahead and around the corner out of sight is the elegant and uncluttered line of the John Lewis department store – formerly Bourne's. Cross the busy road by the pedestrian lights and go straight ahead into Timberhill.

The street itself has some good examples of three-storey houses where the top floor, and especially the windows, seems too large for the overall proportions: as referred to earlier, these top rooms were usually used for the shoe or cloth trade. On your right as you pass down the hill you will encounter The Murderers public house. The story behind the name is disclosed in Walk 11.

At the bottom turning right, you find yourself in front of the Bell Hotel, an old coaching inn, once the meeting place for the infamous 'Hell Fire Club'. It was also a favoured place to book a room if you wanted to be near a public hanging which took place close by. Crowds of up to 30,000 attended these grisly events, the last one being in 1867 when Hubbard Lingley lost his life at the tender age of 22. Hangings continued, but inside the Castle walls. The alternative to hanging was transportation to Australia and between ten and twenty people a year suffered this fate between 1820 and 1840, including an eight-year-old boy who stole two bottles from someone's doorstep.

Straight ahead is one of the great glories of Norwich – the Norman Castle, started by William the Conqueror in 1067 and completed in the main by 1121. There are clear signs

The entrance to Castle Mall off Timberhill

Right: Timberhill

Far right: Little architectural gems, now used as business premises, just off Timberhill

Norwich Castle
(Daniel Tink - www.scenicnorfolk.co.uk)

Old and new: the Norman Castle and latest design in double-deckers

to the entrance and it is worth mentioning that if you only want a quick look around, it is best to go late in the day when the entry charge is drastically reduced.

The main structure stands on a flint base. It is made of Caen stone brought up the River Yare. Originally, the whole 'community' covered over 20 acres and would have had its own workshops, stables, and gatehouses. Today there is just the keep and mound but there is much to see inside. The top floor comprises the grand hall where feasts, meetings and daily business took place. No king ever lived here, but the royal apartments can be seen on the south side. Details of how the common man lived can also be seen – including the communal side-by-side stone toilets (garderobes).

East Anglia's Queen Boudica is celebrated here alongside some exquisite pieces of Iceni gold. Sound and video adds to the experience as you wander around.

Downstairs are the heart-sapping prisons, where those sentenced to hang would spend their last night and petty felons would serve their sentences. Once pronounced legally dead, felons would have a death mask made, of which a collection can be seen in the dungeon. There was, for a time, a belief that the shape of a person's skull could give clues as to personality,

Castle Bridge
(Daniel Tink - www.scenicnorfolk.co.uk)

in particular, inherent criminal tendencies. Thus those hanged should theoretically have similar characteristics, but this does not seem to be the case looking at these specimens. Between 1300 and 1800 the primary use of the Castle was as a prison but it became increasingly overcrowded and eventually, in 1883, the county jail moved to Mousehold Heath.

There is a much more cheerful side to the Castle, too. In 1894, Edward Boardman converted the keep into a museum. Highlights include an extensive and imaginatively mounted 19th century bird collection, an unrivalled range of paintings by the so-called Norwich School of Artists, notably John Crome and John Sell Cotman and a collection of ceramic teapots reputed to be the largest in the world. Over £11 million was spent updating the Castle in 2001 and there are now some good hands-on exhibits, especially popular with children. There is a reasonably priced and comfortable café near the exit.

Junction of Ber Street and All Saints Green before Bournes, now John Lewis, was built

Before leaving the Castle Gardens altogether, you may like to locate some of the fine sculptures dotted around outside. There is 'Sea Form (Atlantic)' by Dame Barbara Hepworth; 'Parrot Head (Rubio)' by Bernard Reynolds and 'Monument to Daedalus' by Jonathan Clarke.

Turn right as you leave the castle – the Bell Hotel will be behind you - and wander around the base of the mound. The pavement soon takes a sharp turn right. Ahead you will see a fine statue of 'Peace', who, with flamboyant wings, is in the process of sheathing her sword to mark the end of hostilities in the Boer War. It was designed by George Wade and erected in 1904, dedicated to the soldiers of Norfolk and Norwich who gave their lives.

Suitably, perhaps, the building on your right just around the corner is the Royal Norfolk Regimental Museum which commemorates a soldier's life in war and peace. Inside are letters and poems, rations packs, personal items and military memorabilia. There is also a special section on World War One and further information on Nurse Edith Cavell. Intriguingly, there is apparently a tunnel which connects the museum to the castle – an escape route should the castle be taken?

This walk ends, and the next starts, in front of the museum.

The statue of Peace sheaths her sword to mark the end of the Boer War. Much worse was to come a few years later with the outbreak of the 'War to End Wars'

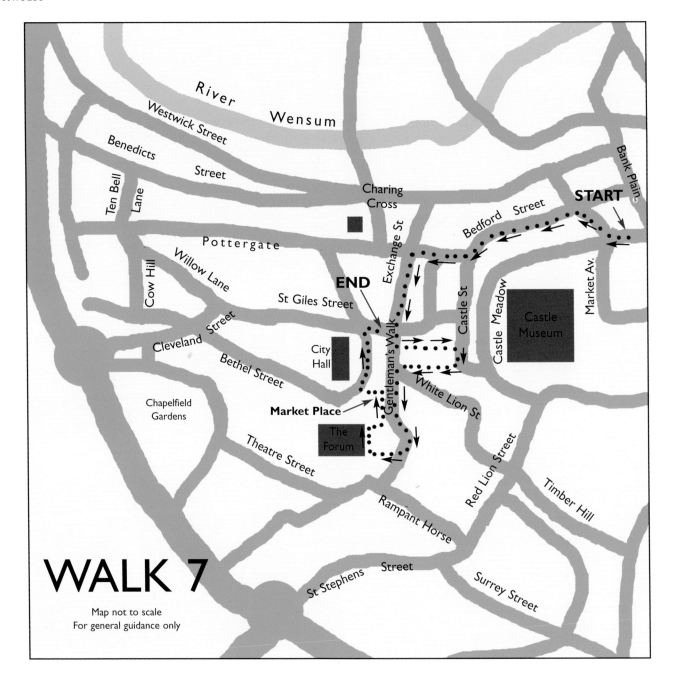

River Wensum

Westwick Street

Benedicts Street

Ten Bell Lane

Charing Cross

Bank Plain

START

Bedford Street

Pottergate

Cow Hill

Willow Lane

Exchange St

END

St Giles Street

Castle St

Castle Meadow

Castle Museum

Market Av.

Cleveland Street

Bethel Street

City Hall

Gentleman's Walk

White Lion St

Chapelfield Gardens

Market Place

The Forum

Red Lion Street

Timber Hill

Theatre Street

Rampant Horse

St Stephens Street

Surrey Street

WALK 7

Map not to scale
For general guidance only

Walk 7

A walk through the centre of town

Walking back a few yards, cross the road, walk down Opie Street and turn left into London Street. Ahead you will see the NatWest Bank which looks more like a Wren Church than a commercial building – it is worth a look inside, too, for it's ornate pillars and plasterwork as well as the central glass dome which floods the banking hall with natural light.

The centre of town can be reached by going down the street either side of the bank, but it is more interesting to go down the cobbled Bedford Street on the right. This is really a continuation of the Lanes and has shops to match – you can buy the last word in HD televisions, exclusive wellington boots, furniture for your home guaranteed no one else will have, or a silver hip-flask engraved with your initials which, filled with an aged malt whisky, will keep you warm when shooting on the moor.

On the corner with Exchange Street is Jarrolds department store. This is one of the few businesses in Norwich still controlled by the original family and is a city institution. You may like to enter through the doors on your left and wander through the very popular book department. If you fancy a coffee, snack or full meal, there is an excellent restaurant on the top floor with fine views over almost the entire area of this walk. Otherwise, leave the store by the doors on your right at the farthest extent of the building, cross the street and look back up to your right. Here can be seen reliefs designed by George Skipper – who designed the store in 1903-5 – and they show aspects of life in the building trades.

You are now standing at the bottom right-hand corner of the main Market Place, the very heart of this old city, and all features of this walk are contained within, or just around, the area you see in front of you. Although the recommended route is a fairly orderly one, that a certain amount of chaos will ensue is probably inevitable: this is because there is so much of interest to see

Can I sing you a song? Entertainer on London Street

George Skipper's depictions of life in the building trade on the side of Jarrolds Department Store

Street entertainers outside Jarrolds Department Store

Shopping in Gentleman's Walk in the run up to Christmas

Entrance to the Royal Arcade

north, south, east and west that any visitor can be forgiven for veering off course now and again.

However, begin by turning left down the wonderfully named Gentleman's Walk. It is a busy and largely pedestrianised area today but, in past centuries, it had a somewhat more rarified air. This is the street where, dressed in their best finery, wigs suitably powdered, perhaps with beauty spot artfully applied, and carrying a silver-topped cane, gentlemen – gentry from the countryside, eminent citizens from other cities, local worthies and assorted 'beaus' – would parade up and down in dignified splendour. Now and again, they would drop into a chop house or coffee shop, the latter more ubiquitous in the 18th and 19th centuries than their modern equivalent, Starbucks, is today. Here, they would read the newspapers, smoke pipes and debate current affairs.

Turn left into Davey Place. This is named after Alderman Jonathan Davey (1760–1814), famous chiefly for holding lots of parties. A businessman called J. Murray also lived here and he set out to halt the bodysnatching business discussed in Walk 6 by selling iron coffins: once sealed and locked, they were said to be impregnable, but the idea failed to really catch on.

Turn right at the crossroad ahead and then right again into The Royal Arcade. This exotic parade is another example of the work of George Skipper in conjunction with a ceramic artist from London by the name of W. J. Neatby. It was built in 1899, restored in 2001, and contains some of the finest art nouveau stained glass, sculpture and tiles in the country. Peacocks strut alongside as you pass the bow-fronted shops. The famous Coleman's Mustard shop is on the left, selling many types of mustard-related products, including quite delicious mustard chocolate. Look up just before you leave the arcade to see a gorgeous art nouveau clock.

The Royal Arcade – an Art Noveau masterpiece

Opposite: Jarrolds on London Street at Christmas
(Daniel Tink - www.scenicnorfolk.co.uk)

A rare lantern slide showing Norwich people out in force on Gentleman's Walk to celebrate the Jubilee in 1897

Fine Art Nouveau Clock and tiling, just above eye level as you leave the Royal Arcade and enter the Market Place

Sir Thomas Browne, a man of considerable erudition and much concerned with the human condition – a sort of 17th century superstar

Turn left and continue your own parade up Gentleman's Walk. Go right on Hay Hill. This is a small open square, very popular with local people for taking a rest from shopping – there are seats and layers of steps to rest on. At top centre, looking, I always think, somewhat bewildered, is a large bronze by Henry Pegram of Sir Thomas Browne. Details can tell us much. Note, for example, the fabulous over-sized bows on his Sir Thomas' shoes: no ordinary man, faced with the everyday problem of walking from A to B amongst the fish heads, ox blood and excrement that flowed in medieval streets would have countenanced such frippery. Here was an important man who spent his travelling time in a carriage. Sir Thomas was born in 1605 and buried a few yards away in St Peter Mancroft church. A very eminent scholar of his time, he wrote several books, his first – *Religio Medici*, concerning the raison d'etre of the medical profession – making him an international figure. King Charles II knighted him on a visit to Norwich in 1671. The new herb garden in the Cloisters is in many ways his legacy as he contributed in no small way to our understanding of the medical and spiritual effects of rosemary, sage and thyme. A modern man? Perhaps, to some degree. Yet, on his advice as a 'specialist' witness, more than one woman is said to have been hanged for witchcraft and bedevilment of youngsters. He died in 1682 but even

The steps leading up from the market past St Peter Mancroft on a cold November morning. Only a quarter of an hour before this photo was taken there was not a snowflake in sight

In 2008, the city was over-run by a herd of colourful elephants, each of which was later sold for charity

then did not find peace. His skull was stolen from his grave in the mid 19th century and only finally reunited with the rest of his mortal remains in 1922.

Walk up past Sir Thomas and St Peter Mancroft Church is on the right. Regarded by many as a church of perfect proportions, and sometimes even mistaken for the Anglican Cathedral, it contrasts strikingly with the glass building to the left of it, Sir Michael Hopkins' Forum. Here is a visual definition of ancient and modern.

St Peter Mancroft is discussed in Walk 10. For now, pass up the slope towards the tiered steps of the performing area in front of the Forum. This is really a mini open-air amphitheatre where all sorts of free events take place at lunchtimes and weekends: in the winter months, an ice rink is set up here. At any time during fine weather, you will see people sitting around chatting and having a snack – the market is just below and food is available at very good prices.

One of the most dramatic photographs that can be taken in Norwich presents itself here as the glass wall of the Forum wonderfully reflects aspects of St Peter Mancroft opposite.

Norwich has boasted a library of sorts since 1608. It was the first city in the UK to do this. Of course, it was restricted to the gentry in those days – let common people have knowledge and who knows what might happen? The present building replaced the Norwich Central Library which was destroyed by fire in 1994. It is horse-shoe shaped and has won several top architectural awards since being opened by Queen Elizabeth II in 2002. The bricks are handmade.

The Forum
(Daniel Tink - www.scenicnorfolk.co.uk)

It is not, however, a traditional library in the sense of a quiet place to read and study. Rather, as it is called the Forum, which means 'meeting place' in Latin, it is designed to be used by citizens in many ways. You can have a coffee, pizza or beer here; you can wander around the many – and often noisy - exhibitions in the Atrium; you can shop for souvenirs; you can bring your baby or toddler along to a 'sing-in'; and you can, of course, take out books and CDs. Some people express dissatisfaction with this as they do not know what to make of it and it is true that it can be frustrating to try to find a quiet place to study: the open-plan of the entire building does not help. Best to go to either UEA Library – photographic proof of identity and letter confirming local address needed – or to the Cathedral Library if you are looking for a haven of peace and quiet.

Passing into the large and bright Atrium, you will see a café on the ground floor and a restaurant looking out from the first. The BBC has a regional headquarters here also. The downstairs part of the Forum contains an impressive collection of CDs – films and music. At the back is the 2nd Air Division USAAF Memorial Library, set up to commemorate the hundreds of missions flown by the United States Eighth Air Force during the Second World War. There were 14 heavy bomber airfields in Norfolk and Suffolk as well as five fighter airfields and almost seven thousand American airmen gave their lives during the war. This is also a fine spot for reading American magazines and selecting books on most aspects of life in the USA.

There is a lift as well as stairs to the two other floors. On the first are contained the bulk of the books for hire as well as a comfortable seating area where people sit to read the day's newspapers or latest magazines. The second floor is a business, local history and heritage centre where many spend time tracing the family tree. You will see, on both floors, dozens of state-of-the-art computers which are free to use once you have joined the library.

Above: The BBC has its regional headquarters in the Forum

Far Left: The Forum hosts many exhibitions

Middle: A robot dances in the Atrium of the Forum as a plant sale goes on around him

Fireworks explode over the city centre to mark the beginning of the Christmas celebration
(Daniel Tink - www.scenicnorfolk.co.uk)

The market stalls have all been replaced in recent years but the vibrant colours have been retained

To the left of the Forum as you come out is the very heart of the city – the Market Place. The temporary stalls have been upgraded in the last few years – now they are permanent structures which still retain the traditional colourful striped roofs. Retractable glass panels above the walkways ingeniously protect shoppers when it is wet.

There has been a market here since the time of William the Conqueror. Records show that it was the centre for the sale of meat, fish and fruit and later came to be important for shoe mending, silks, linen, leather goods and cheap bread, sometimes of dubious quality. Early records show that the City Council wanted it to be a food-only market. This was certainly how much of the population saw it. Norwich Biscuits would have been sold, simple to make and designed to fill you up at minimum expense. Here is the recipe:

Ingredients
8 oz flour
4 oz sugar
¼ oz ginger OR 2 oz chopped local apples
2 oz lard
2 oz treacle (or Golden Syrup today)
2 oz water

Method
Mix together. Cut into biscuits. Bake for 10 minutes

You can make these more tasty by adding other chopped fruit or raisins.

Although many other businesses thrive today, it is still largely seen by the locals as a somewhere to eat. This is a favourite place to buy mugs of tea and all sorts of food – giant bacon sandwiches, hog roast rolls, chicken chow mien, fish and chips, meat pie and mushy

Right: A busy shopping morning: looking up at the Market from Gentleman's Walk

Far right: A colourful corner of the Market

peas, speciality cheeses, Norfolk ice-cream and lots more. Browsing for second-hand books, records or videos can also be rewarding.

Recently, I hosted an eminent historian from an overseas university. I asked her 'if you could go back several centuries, what would be your overwhelming impression of this place: the buildings, the hustle and bustle, the affluence of the city - what?' She said 'My main impression would be of smell. A modern person would faint. The sanitation was dreadful or non-existent, and people didn't wash much - faced with a multitude of other worries, why bathe? What kind of a waste of time was that?'

The market has, in addition, been the centre for maintaining 'discipline' in the local population. Following Kett's rebellion, forty-five of his lieutenants were hanged, drawn and quartered here. If you were a man and caught in rowdy or drunken behaviour, you would like as not spend an uncomfortable few hours in the market place stocks, perhaps be placed in a cage without food and water or take a lashing whilst tied to a whipping post. Women would generally be sentenced to punishment by ducking stool, notably at Fye Bridge as previously mentioned.

City Hall

Overlooking the Market Place is the 'new' City Hall, opened by George VI in 1938. The famous architectural historian, Nikolas Pevsner, liked it a great deal, but others have not been so sure. Locals sometimes mockingly describe it as having the complexion of 'Brown Windsor Soup'. It seems Lord Haw-Haw didn't like it much either as he claimed at the height of the Blitz that it was soon to be destroyed by German bombers. We are spoilt in Norwich, having so many buildings, mostly ancient but some modern ones, too, that are exceptional and so perhaps the architects (Charles Holloway James and Stephen Rowland Pierce) were on a hiding to nothing when trying to please everyone. My opinion is that it is a fine art deco structure that provides a happy contrast to the previous centre of government – the medieval Guildhall – which lies just below it.

Two fine art-deco lions flank the main entrance. One of these was spotted by the architects at the British Empire Exhibition in 1936 and a matching pair was ordered from designer, Alfred Hardiman. The doors are made of bronze and feature 18 plaques by James Woodward commemorating the main trades of the city – including shoe, beer, chocolate and mustard production. On some days in the year the public is allowed to climb the one-hundred-and-sixty-six steps to the viewing platform at the top of the clock tower.

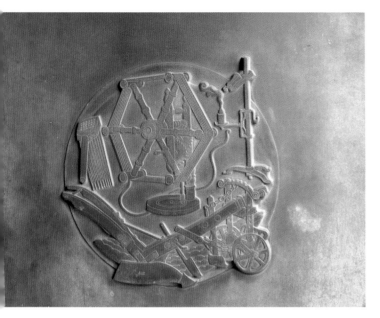

Above: One design on the doors of City Hall, each of which depicts a Norwich trade

Above right: One of a pair of lions, spotted by the architects at the British Empire Exhibition in 1936, keeps guard over the entrance to City Hall. They cost a fortune in their day. The old town hall can be seen in the background

The main hall is well worth a look for the classic art deco interior.

Leaving the main entrance of City Hall, you will see just down the slope on the left the ancient Guildhall. It is both a fine building with some attractive squared and diamond-shaped flint work, and a bit of a fraud, too, as the authentic-looking clock tower is, in fact, Victorian. It was started in 1407 as the city was getting a high opinion of itself by this time and needed a more prestigious headquarters than the existing Toll House. Labour was no problem as special constables were empowered to 'press' anyone they chose into working up to 15 hours a day on the project. The prison was in the vaults. It was here that the most famous of the Norwich martyrs, Thomas Bilney, was held before being burnt at the stake. The Courts also sat here, as did the Council. Today, you can have tea while imagining all the important decisions being made, and harsh sentences being meted out, exactly where you sit and sup.

Just like the Anglican Cathedral, the Guildhall suffered from construction problems as, in 1511, the roof collapsed and, in 1635, the hall became unsafe due to the saltpetre mining being carried on around it. The hand of man almost destroyed it in 1911 when a motion was put to the Council that it was too expensive to maintain and, furthermore, it was wrong to preserve something just because it was old. This was only narrowly defeated. Thus both

Elm Hill and the Guildhall, two of the city's most loved architectural treasures, share a bond in that both only just managed to survive the politicians and their so-called 'progressive' policies.

This walk ends here and leaves you at leisure in the very centre of town.

Colourful signs and haircut to match on Gaol Hill

As fine an example of knapped flint as you will ever see: the original Town Hall built, in large part, by 'pressed' labour: if you walked past here when it was being built without your wits about you, you might find yourself part of the building team

A snow storm does its best to cover the pavement, post box opposite City Hall and market rooftops in a blanket of white

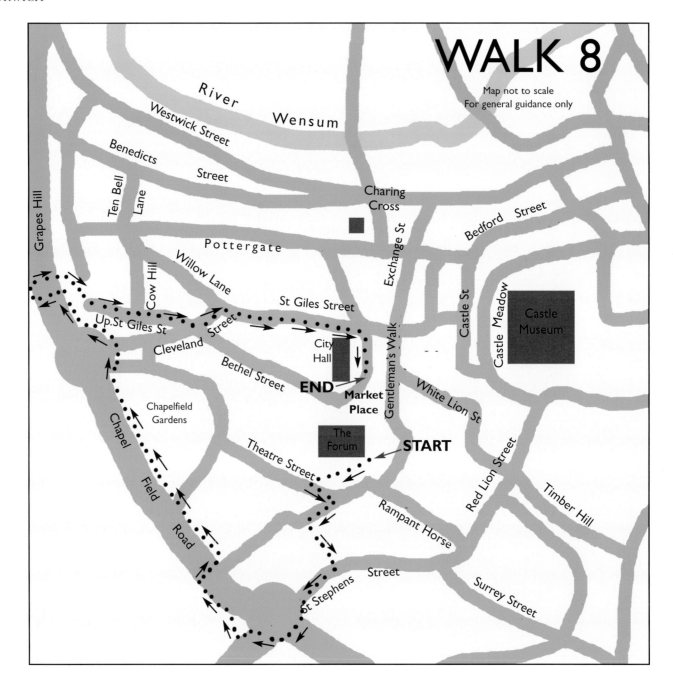

WALK 8

Map not to scale
For general guidance only

River
Wensum
Westwick Street
Benedicts
Street
Ten Bell
Lane
Grapes Hill
Charing
Cross
Bedford Street
Exchange St
Pottergate
Cow Hill
Willow Lane
St Giles Street
Castle St
Castle Meadow
Castle Museum
Up.St Giles St
Street
Cleveland
City
Hall
Gentleman's Walk
Bethel Street
END
Market
Place
White Lion St
Chapel
Chapelfield
Gardens
The
Forum
START
Red Lion Street
Field
Theatre Street
Rampant Horse
Timber Hill
Road
St Stephens
Street
Surrey Street

Walk 8

A walk taking in the Chapelfield Shopping Centre, St Stephens Gate, some of the city walls, Chapelfield Gardens, the Cathedral Church of St John the Baptist and the Victorian Plantation Gardens

Leaving the Forum, turn right and first left into Rampant Horse Street. Cut through the churchyard of St Stephen's Church and into the city's latest multi-million pound retail development – Chapelfield Centre. As shopping malls go, this is certainly up there with the best – it is bright and light with wide avenues between the shops. The other indoor centre, Castle Mall, is cramped and claustrophobic by comparison. House of Fraser is here as is a huge Borders bookshop on two floors. There is an interesting selection of goods on sale, too – fine teas, handmade soaps, almost irresistible chocolate, bagels filled however you wish, cameras, sports goods, chemists products and, naturally, lots of fashion for men and women. On the top floor is a surprisingly pleasant and varied food hall.

Chapelfield centre was opened in 2005. A survey by a major credit card company in 2006 put Norwich city centre as number one in the UK as regards customer satisfaction.

Far left: Entrance to Chapelfield Shopping Centre

Below: A highly original clock design on the side of Chapelfield Shopping Centre

Caley's – a famous Norwich brand

A pub sign in Chapelfield Road reminding us that boxing bouts were big business in the 18th and 19th century

Chapelfield Centre is on the site previously occupied by Caley's chocolate, at one time a famous Norwich company. Caleys began as a producer of mineral water before diversifying into chocolate and Christmas crackers. The factory was bombed and set badly ablaze in the Second World War, but the firm recovered. It was sold several times, ending up with Nestlé who transferred all production to York in 1996, a sad day for Norwich as it ended 120 years of chocolate production. Happily, Caleys chocolate is now being made again in Norwich.

When you have had your fill of shopping, take the elevator to the ground floor and leave by the St Stephens Street entrance. Turn right and walk past the shops to the roundabout and cross straight ahead by using the underground walkway. You are now in St Stephens Road. Look up to your right for a remarkable three-dimensional representation – a cross between a model and a painting of St Stephens Gate at the time of Charles II. It was made by Mr John Moray-Smith and unveiled in November 1937. Turn back and left up Chapelfield Road. On your left is the Champion pub with a fine sign which once again illustrates the importance of bare-knuckle boxing to the city in general and pubs in particular. An exceptionally good view of the old city walls can also be seen from here – the best stretch there is. With the modern flats that were built as part of Chapelfield immediately behind the ruins, here is a view of both the oldest and the most modern aspects of the city.

Ahead on the left is Chapelfield Methodist Church – well worth a separate visit if you have time – and, in front, is a pedestrian crossing. Using this to cross the road, the walk now goes inside the city walls and you thus have a close up of the ancient flintwork on your left and the fine new flats on your right.

At the top of the road you pass through some ornate black metal gates. This is now Chapelfield Gardens with some fine vistas and even finer trees. There is a bandstand in the

Fellowes Plain – a conversion of the old Norfolk and Norwich hospital building into elegant flats

A fine stretch of the old wall alongside the Chapelfield development

Chapelfield Gardens in the Spring
(Daniel Tink - www.scenicnorfolk.co.uk)

Above: Fine tree-lined walkway in Chapelfield Gardens

Above far right: The Cathderal of St John the Baptist

Elegant iron balconies front these houses alongside Chapelfield Gardens

middle, much used on Victorian Sunday afternoons when a selection of suitably uplifting hymns would be played. It was also reputed to be a centre for compulsory archery practice during the 13th and 14th centuries and the training given here must have contributed to the famous victory at Agincourt in 1415. Walking straight ahead you will pass a café and a childrens' play area. It is best to leave by the bottom right exit as this minimises the risks from the exceptionally heavy traffic on the roundabout ahead as you make your way to the Roman Catholic Cathedral. Cross the road to your right and carry straight on until you come to a footbridge that will take you over Grapes Hill dual carriageway.

You are now on Earlham Road and the Cathedral Church of St John the Baptist rises majestically in front of you.

The instigating force behind this fine building was Henry, 15th Duke of Norfolk (1847–1917). He wanted to restore the Roman Catholic faith to the pre-eminence it once enjoyed. Considering himself to be truly blessed following his happy marriage to Lady Flora Hastings in 1877, he wished to build a great church as a 'thank-you' to God.

The church was designed by George Gilbert Scott and the site chosen that of the old city gaol, a place apparently so black and daunting that children did not like to walk by it. There were many problems during the construction – it was discovered that ancient chalk works weakened the site and, when, building began ten years later, the stone used – Devon Beer – was found to weather badly and new stone had to be found. Today, the visitor is struck by the surprising wear and tear in some outside parts of the building: The Anglican Cathedral is eight hundred years older and yet the Caen stone is in far finer condition. The Duke also suffered the loss of his wife at the tender age of 34 and his son and heir was born blind. However, he persevered with his dream and eventually, in 1910, the church was opened.

During the Second World War the church, built on some of the highest land in Norwich, was used as a beacon by the American bombers returning to their East Anglian bases from raids on Europe. It must have been a lovely sight in the night sky, made doubly beautiful due to the crew's safe return.

In 1976 the Pope announced the setting up of the Diocese of East Anglia and the church of St John the Baptist became a Cathedral.

The intricate metalwork on the external doors gives an insight into what will be found inside – everywhere, the carving is detailed and rich producing an overall impression of French Gothic splendour. The carvings are medieval in subject – birds, flowers, devils – but, being Victorian, they are somewhat chaste in their details. There is a preponderance of

Thousands of fossilized creatures can be seen in every pillar made of Durham marble in the Roman Catholic Cathedral

Far left: A memorial – this one is at Norwich International Airport – to the many brave American servicemen who flew from this area and gave their lives in the Second World War

Left: Rich and splendid – the interior of the Cathedral

pillars made of dark Durham marble in which can be seen thousands of fossilised creatures. The ten bays in the nave are supported by massive columns. Looking down from the west end, you will see that the chancel is slightly off-centre – this is because it represents Christ on the cross with his head slightly to one side. A touching feature is the memorial to the people of Poland, 1939–45, who fled to Norwich and, from here, fought back against their oppressors. Norwich has had a thriving Polish community ever since.

It is believed that Henry, 15th Duke of Norfolk, designed the window in the north transept which pictures the Queen of Heaven with the Christ Child.

Gwendolen, the second wife of the 15th Duke, donated the Walsingham chapel in the north-east corner. The Blessed Sacrament chapel on the south side is set aside for private prayer.

There is some fine stained glass here – see the great West Window dedicated, naturally, to St John the Baptist. Enemy bombers were responsible for extensive damage during the war but most has been expertly restored, often from the existing plans – one great advantage of having a relatively new church.

The tower is open to visitors on Saturdays in summer at 1.30 and 2.30. A modest charge is made and booking in advance from the Tourist Information Centre is advised. Vertigo sufferers should avoid this trip at all costs – for others, the views over the city and surroundings are unparalleled.

Mass is celebrated at 10.00 am Monday to Friday, at 6.00 pm on Saturday and at 9.00 am and 11.00 am on Sunday.

Below: The beautiful Plantation Gardens

Far right: Detail of the original intricate stonework in the gardens

There is a shop which sells a guide to the cathedral with more stories ,and details about future plans for this very much alive and thriving place. Educational trips are encouraged – teachers should email: education@stjohncathedral.co.uk

Only a few yards separate the cathedral from the next stop on the walking tour. The Plantation Garden is often referred to by locals as 'the secret garden' and it does have a magical quality. You step into it by walking down the gently sloping bank next to the Beeches Hotel, on the Earlham Road and, if it is not manned as is quite likely, you put your £2 entrance fee in the honesty - red post office – box. As you pass through the small entry gate the twenty-first century gives way to the 1900s.

An elegant building in St Giles Street

The garden was designed by Henry Trevor, a wealthy Norwich cabinet maker and upholsterer, between 1856 and 1896. It was a Victorian country-house garden in miniature with fancy brickwork, fountain, instant 'ruins', and follies. In all it consists of only 3 acres and yet, with its circular routes set on several different levels, it feels as if you are walking in a grand country estate. Originally, there was also a Palm House with hot water pipes and exotic plants, but this is gone now. Original black and white photographs show how intricate were the flower planting schemes.

Mr Trevor was very proud of his garden, welcoming its use by charitable causes and so it must have been a well known local feature in the early days. Unfortunately, during the Second World War the garden was totally neglected. Forty years later the Plantation Garden Preservation Trust began work to clear the weeds and ivy. The present fine state of the garden is entirely down to their hard work. You can join the Trust for £7.50 per year - £12 for families - which includes free entry and notification of special ticket-only events such as the annual Summer Fete and Autumn Guy Fawkes Party. Sir Roy Strong is Patron.

When you have finished walking, taking photographs and, perhaps eating your picnic meal, leave the garden and carry on back the way you came. When you have re-crossed the dual carriageway by the bridge and reached the top of Upper St Giles Street, you may like to bear left down St Giles Street which will lead you, past some fine eating houses – including a restaurant specialising in savoury and sweet waffles and one in fine fish – to the Market Place and Forum, where this walk began.

The black, red and blue routes are suggestions for walks around the area in which it is possible to wander freely around the Broad and in the parkland.

Earlham Hall School of Law

END

START

SPORTS PARK

River Yare

EARLHAM PARK

Uinversity Drive

UNIVERSITY OF EAST ANGLIA

Blue Bell Road

NORWICH AND NORFOLK UNIVERSITY HOSPITAL

Colney Lane

Sainsbury Centre

BROAD

Colney Lane

Woodland

Norwich Bypass

Colney Lane

CRINGLEFORD

WALK 9

Newmarket Road

Bypass

To Danby Wood

Cringleford

Map not to scale
For general guidance only

Walk 9

A walk around the 320-acre campus of the University of East Anglia, including the University Broad, the Yare Valley Walk, Earlham Park and the Sportspark

This walks commences on the campus of the University of East Anglia. By car it is basically straight up the Earlham Road – the Cathedral Church of St John the Baptist marks the city end – until you see UEA signposted off to your left and you enter University Drive. Buses offer a 24 hour service to and from the same location, and run about every 15 minutes from Castle Meadow.

UEA has just over 15,000 undergraduates and over 4,000 postgraduates, with a large contingent coming from overseas, especially Asia. Academically, UEA has a growing international reputation. It is currently placed about 20th in the major surveys of national standing. The School of Creative Writing has produced three Booker Prize winners: Anne Enright for *The Gathering* in 2007; Kazuo Ishiguro, who is probably best known for *Remains of the Day* which became a much-praised film starring Sir Anthony Hopkins; and Ian McEwan who wrote, among many other novels, *Atonement*, which was also turned into a major international film starring Kiera Knightly and James MacAvoy. Among a long list of distinguished alumni in other fields are Sir Paul Nurse, who won the 2001 Nobel Prize in Physiology or Medicine; Tito Mboweni, present head of the South African Reserve Bank; Baroness Amos, past Leader of the House of Lords; and Rear Admiral Neil Morisetti, Commander of UK Maritime Forces.

UEA is, of course, the premier university in the whole of East Anglia and thus, as it is based in Norwich, the city can rightly claim a connection with one of the country's leading composers, Benjamin Britten. Although strictly a Suffolk man having been born in Lowestoft and schooled in Holt, the composer of some of the most sublime pieces in the classical canon is commemorated in the name of a university students' residential hall. Britten composed over 800 pieces as a young man before the War Requiem brought him international fame. He worked with many 20th century literary and artistic 'greats', including WH Auden. He was a modest man and claimed late in life that his work never reached the ultimate heights, a verdict not shared by practically everyone else. Having previously declined a knighthood, he accepted the title of Baron Britten shortly before his death in 1976, the first time such an honour has been bestowed upon a composer.

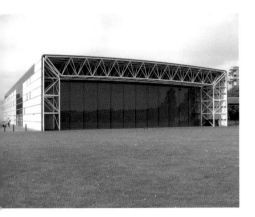

Lord Foster's Sainsbury Centre – as it is a sunny day, people have taken their drinks outside the café to the left

UEA has the motto 'Do Different', which is reflected in the innovative curriculum offered, often employing an interdisciplinary approach where subjects are taught as far as possible in relation to each other.

The campus dates from 1960 and was designed in the main by Sir Denys Lasdun. One of the defining features is that the teaching facilities are contained in a continuous teaching wall that runs from west to east. When you arrive, walk down the gentle slope of University Drive and then Chancellor's Drive until you see a sign for the Sainsbury Centre for Visual Arts, at the western end of the teaching wall. This was one of the early works by Norman Foster who went on to become one of the greatest of world architects having in recent years designed, among many other famous buildings, Beijing International Airport. In the 1980s, Lord Foster was asked to extend the building as more space was needed for exhibits, and this he did by building, not on the side, but underneath the existing cuboid structure. The result – looking back at it from the River Yare – is what looks like a hill of green grass with a glass storey in the middle.

The Sainsbury Centre houses the art collection of Sir Robert and Lady Lisa Sainsbury. Much of the display comes from Africa, Asia and North and South America. On the lawns outside, are artworks and sculptures by eminent artists including Francis Bacon, Jacob Epstein and Henry Moore. All this is free to see. The centre also usually has another exhibition running simultaneously which is not free.

There are two entrances to the Centre on the university side. Both lead to cafés, one of which is large and quite traditional in its menu – quiche, salads, sandwiches, rolls, a special hot course meal, tea, coffee etc at reasonable prices. The other is more continental in flavour, selling items like cous-cous with fresh salad dressed in olive oil, ciabatta sandwiches, several varieties of home-made sponge sandwich cakes, fresh fruit and a selection of teas. This latter overlooks the free art collection and is a relaxing place to take a break.

Right: State-of-the-art accommodation is essential to attract overseas students

Far right: Sculptures by eminent artists dot the campus

Walk around the Centre – or, if the weather is fine the glass doors from the 'continental' café will be open – and down the slope towards the lake. Look back for a fine view of the famous 'ziggurats' of Sir Denys Lasdun, now Grade II listed. It is a shame that such a striking architectural vision had to be curtailed in the 1970s due to lack of finance. A cheaper building – the unloved Waveney Terrace – was constructed alongside. This was demolished in 2006 and some new accommodation has recently been completed. Each colourful and elegant block has been named after such eminent men as Horatio Nelson, John Constable, Benjamin Britten, Jeremiah Coleman, Nelson's flagship HMS *Victory*, Robert Kett, Sir Thomas Browne and the Paston family. UEA has invested much effort in recruiting students from overseas and, for this, state-of-the-art accommodation is essential.

The famous 'ziggurats' of Sir Denys Lasdun

Looking back you can see these superb buildings and the ziggurats set against the sky on a rising hill – it makes a fine picture.

You are now coming to the University Broad, which was formed in the 1970s when gravel was extracted for building work. One idea is to walk completely around it, taking in the wildlife and lovely views back towards the university. There are seats at regular intervals. Another is to walk around the Broad to the far side and take one of the several different paths that open up. There is, for example, a small bridge on the near corner to where you are standing . Passing across the bridge will take you to thick woodland where you can wander. In spring this is a mass of bluebells, and in autumn a rich riot of reds, browns and greens. Although popular with locals, sometimes with their dogs, the area is so large that chances are you or your party may not see another soul.

Far left: In Spring and Summer the area is a riot of wild flowers which 'intoxicate with their beauty', to quote the late Spike Milligan

Left: Sun-dappled pathway on the edge of Earlham Park

Above: View of the Broad from the university

Above right: A view back from the far side of the Broad towards the university

Thick woods within a few minutes' walk of the campus

An alternative is to turn left and follow the Yare Valley Walk for almost as many miles as you like. It continues past the farthest extent of the Broad, into Eaton, past Marston Marsh and ends in Danby Wood, where there is a car park. You are just off the Ipswich Road here, not far from the city centre.

My personal favourite, however, is to turn right at this point and follow the stream. You will see that the water is absolutely clear and thousands of fish can be seen darting about. The walk has fascination for the naturalist at any time of the year – the sea cabbages and other strange looking plants on the banks and in the stream, meadows of celandines (Wordsworth's favourite flower – not daffodils as most people think), swathes of bright yellow rises, waterboatmen, huge dragonflies in metallic hues of blue and turquoise, and pink, white and yellow waterlilies. Here, too, are nesting swans, ducks and shrill-sounding waterhens.

You will pass some sports fields on your left and cross over a small road. The path is clearly made out and you will find yourself in a damp wood. Carry on walking and, almost out of the blue, you will see a brightly lit exit among the trees. You have come to Earlham Park.

If you stop and look at the upward-sloping fields with ancient oak trees scattered here and there and, in spring and summer, a covering of wild flowers in hues of white, yellow, blue and mauve, you may imagine that you have stepped into the pages of a Thomas Hardy novel. The fattest rabbits you ever saw, quite unconcerned by your presence, hop about and nibble the grass. The 'University Village' is at the far side of the park and students use the fields as the most direct route to lectures.

If you wander across the park, you will find a café. Earlham Hall itself is now the UEA School of Law.

The River Yare

Strolling along the River Yare

In Spring the area is covered in bluebells

Have you ever seen a more inviting path?

Swans preen themselves on the river: the background is a picture of wild buttercups and celandines

Entrance to Earlham Park in Spring

Clematis-covered wall and archway in Earlham Park

A perfect spot to take some exercise

Ducks by the broad

*A wisteria-covered archway in
Earlham Park*

A formal corner of Earlham Park, perfect for a picnic

Earlham Hall itself is now the UEA Faculty of Law

Exiting to the right of Earlham Hall and walking back towards the university proper – it is clearly signed – you come to the Sportspark, one of the biggest multi-sports facilities in the country and built in 2001. It is fully open to the public. For about £4 you can use the Bernard Matthews Olympic Swimming Pool: often you have it almost all to yourself. When you have finished your swim, you can eat at the café in the complex which serves fresh and healthy food at very good prices. The café is alongside a climbing wall on the one side and a running track of international standard on another. These facilities are almost constantly in use and make an unusual backdrop to your meal.

Leaving the Sportspark and carrying on towards the university proper, you will come within a few minutes to the centre of the campus. Sir Denys Lasdun designed the buildings so that none should be more than five minutes from another and this principle has been broadly followed since. Thus, you will soon be standing in front of the Union Pub and Bar, a most impressive and comfortable ale house which has recently undergone a million pound refit. There are other bars and cafés scattered around, as well as general food shops, banks and a Waterstone's bookshop. In fine weather, students will be sitting on the rows of steps chatting, eating or studying for the upcoming seminar.

The University Library is well worth a visit and an excellent place for quiet study. You need to produce a proof of a Norwich address and photographic ID.

If you need to take a bus back to town they leave regularly, 24 hours a day, from the Chancellor's Drive.

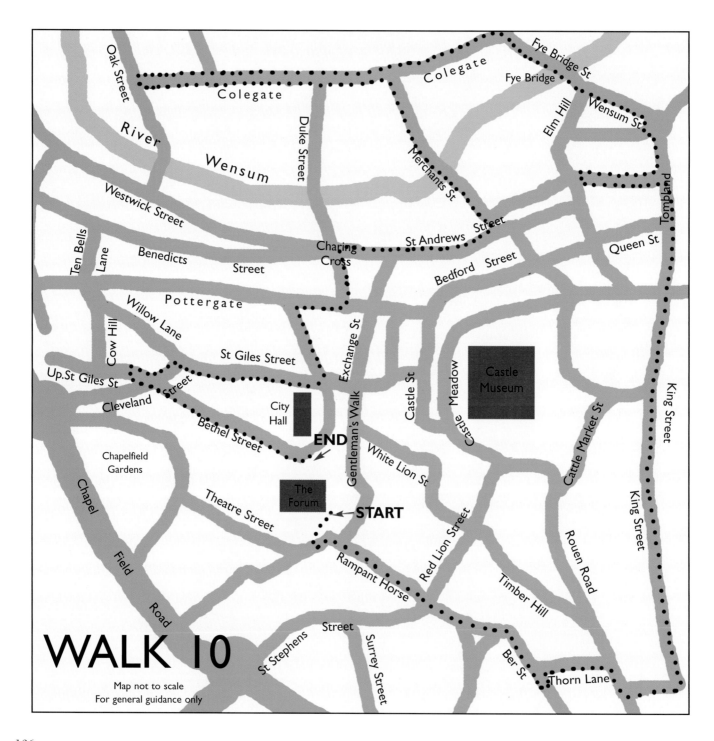

WALK 10

Map not to scale
For general guidance only

Walk 10

A walk around 17 notable churches

Norwich has two cathedrals: the Anglican and the Roman Catholic, both covered in previous walks. It also has 31 beautiful medieval churches. Unfortunately, only nine of these are used for regular worship, although some have been converted to other uses. There used to be more. We have no idea how many there were 1500 years ago as they were generally made of wood and were constantly being destroyed, pulled down and put up somewhere else. Much better records were kept when flint and stone came to be used in the construction, and we know that, prior to AD1500, Norwich was legendary for having more churches that London, York and Bristol combined, as many as 53. First, the Jews and later, in the 16th century, the Flemish weavers who came over to escape persecution, led to a strong tradition of religious tolerance and 'dissent' from orthodox religious thinking – hence 'Dissenters' – and swelled the number of chapels in the city. The exact number depends on how you wish to define a church. Hence Daniel Defoe counted 32 in 1722 whilst Corbridge's Plan in 1727 shows 35 conventional churches – ie those with a spire or tower plus a nave – within the city walls. Some, such as St Julian, were damaged in Hitlers 'Baedeker Raids', named after the guide books which the Nazis used to decide which cities to bomb, aiming to maximise distress and collapse of morale by destroying the finest of England's architectural gems. Great damage was inflicted generally on Norwich during the Second World War.

To the medieval mind, the relative size of the congregation or the amount of use were not the most important things. Building a fine church was in itself an act of worship and generation after generation would employ their after-work skills on a particular church – the family project, as it were. Often, they were financed by benefactors keen to leave a monument to themselves. If a church was not used, well, it was still there as you walked down the street, wasn't it? In parts of the city there is one every few hundred yards, and just looking at it made you think of God. Many assume that the lack of use for churches is a modern-day phenomenon and yet records show that Norwich has always had, as we see it, 'too many churches'. But we think about them with a different mindset today, a largely financial one, it has to be said. One of the causes of our present attitude is that far less people nowadays believe in God: a recent survey showed that almost 28% of Norwich citizens have no religious faith – the highest percentage of any city in the land.

St Swithin's Arts Centre

St Michael-at-Plea – another imaginative alternative use for a church – this one is a bookshop and restaurant

Of course, redundant churches cost a great deal to keep up. Many and varied have been the schemes to pay for them. Conversion of use is one such – thus we have churches used as a craft market (St Gregory), an arts centre (St Swithin), a science centre (St Michael of Coslany), an art gallery (St Margaret), a printing works (St Mary Coslany), a community centre and café (All Saints Centre), a concert hall and market (St Andrew and Blackfriars), a puppet theatre (St James Whitefriars), a painting studio (St Ethelreda) and a bookshop and café (St Michael-at-Plea). Some, however, like St Laurence, look very sad and bereft with a chain and padlock on the gates.

Flint, of which many Norwich churches are built , looks black and unpleasant if neglected. In the 1940s it was suggested that, as it was the wealth of industry which originally paid for them, churches should be 'adopted' by prosperous local firms. This may been popular with the medieval barons but has not been so well-received in more modern times. On occasions in the early part of the last century exasperation took hold and local politicians simply suggested they be knocked down. Luckily, they mostly remain but future financing continues to be a pressing worry.

St James Whitefriars – now a puppet theatre

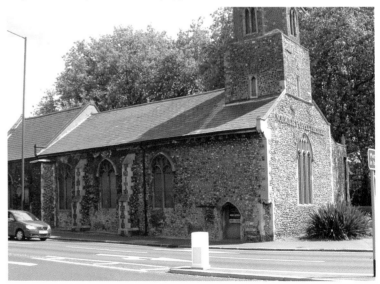

Far left: A visual definition of ancient and modern – the Forum and St Peter Mancroft

Left: Looking out from the steps of City Hall towards St Peter Mancroft during a snow blizzard

This walk starts at St Peter Mancroft, opposite the Forum. The first mystery of this exceptionally fine church is the name – there is no St Peter Mancroft. Probably – no one knows with absolute certainty – the name derives from 'Magna Crofta' which means 'Great Meadow', upon which the church was built in the years 1430–55. The 'Saint' part probably derives from the original name – St Peter and St Paul. Thus: 'St Peter on the Great Meadow'.

So lovely are the proportions, and so large, that visitors from outside the area have been known to mistake the church for the Anglican Cathedral. John Wesley, who knew about these things, wrote that he had never seen a more beautiful parish church. Of course, he would have seen it before the unfortunate addition of the pepper castors and lead-covered flèche plonked on the top by George Street, R.A., in 1883. Wesley also said something else that strikes the visitor when standing at the West End and looking down the high and bright aisle – it is a 'surprisingly cheerful' place.

There is much to detain you here and there is sometimes a guide on duty who will be happy to answer questions. The brightness is helped by the windows to the North and South sides. The East Window is magnificent, made entirely of 15th-century Norwich glass. The roof is of timber supported by hammer beams. Hard to believe that, in the 1960s, it had to be raised and put back again after the walls, bulging under the weight, were strengthened and straightened.

Stained glass window in St Peter Mancroft

There are two organs, the oldest being the East End organ, dating from 1707. The second is the West End organ of recent (1984) construction but entirely mechanical in operation. It is made of oak with limewood decorations.

Look back from the middle of the aisle and note the archway to the Ringing Tower. There are 14 bells which ring one of the finest peals anywhere in the world. Many times have the bells rung out to celebrate important events in history – we know, for example, that the citizens of Norwich were thus alerted to the defeat of the Spanish Armada in 1588.

The top line of figures in the Reredos behind the altar was carved in 1885 and the lower in 1930, at which time they were both gilded. To the right of the High Altar is a memorial to Sir Thomas Browne, discussed in Walk 7.

Cross the Nave and you will see St Nicholas Chapel which contains what is called the Mancroft Heritage – religious treasures.

Many famous citizens, often Lord Mayors, have memorial plaques on the church walls. One of great interest, from which hangs a fascinating tale, is to be found on the north wall. This commemorates the life of Sir James Smith, founder of the still thriving Linnaeun Society. It was Carl Linnaeus (1707–78) who invented a new method of classifying plants which was also later used for animals. Earlier botanists had tried to classify plants by characteristics such as colour or the shape of leaves. Linnaeus did it according to their reproductive organs. Botany is consequently filled with sexual references. Linnaeus claimed the system was so

The Reredos in St Peter Mancroft

simple that 'even women could understand it'. For a time there was great opposition to his scheme from the narrow-minded British public and much debate in the press about the possible corruption of women and children. Linnaeus worked in conjunction with Sir Joseph Banks who sailed around the world with Captain Cook and collected exotic and unusual plants. Between them they transformed Kew Gardens in London into the world's finest botanical garden, a position it still holds. Banks also established a botanical garden in Calcutta. He is also credited with helping persuade the British government that Australia was worth colonising. He visited Norwich sometimes and gave lectures here. One of his residences was in nearby Lincoln, by the castle.

Leaving the church, walk slightly up hill, first left and then left again into Rampant Horse Street. Opposite is the Church of St Stephen, notable for having a tower on the side, not the front. It is often open for coffee. Dating from 1350, the structure has undergone many changes. Now the churchyard has been pressed into service as the main walkway from Rampant Horse Street into the new Chapelfield Shopping Centre. It is worth a slight detour to see the new gates at the far side: these are very stylish with some of the curved metal bars having rough rocks on them and others coloured translucent orbs. St Stephen was the first Christian martyr and the rocks represent his death by stoning and the orbs jewels on his immortal crown. Beautiful.

Among the many monuments inside is one to Samuel Bignold (1791–1875), son of the founder of Norwich Union. His father, Thomas was somewhat cantankerous. He is reputed to have refused insurance to a man he disliked who wanted cover against being bitten by a mad dog on the grounds that, should a dog do this, then the dog would assuredly be sane. He was forced to retire after a shareholders' revolt and Samuel took over for the next sixty years. The firm went from strength to strength and Samuel, despite many people thinking that such an important firm should be in London, remained resolutely loyal to Norwich. He knew Lord Douro, son of the Duke of Wellington and MP for Norwich, and advised Disraeli on financial matters. He failed, however, to get into Parliament himself.

Carry straight on down to the crossroads and head up Westlegate. At the top on the left is All Saints Centre (officially All Saints Westlegate), a fine little church which has been converted inside into a café and social centre. It is more like a large living room than a church with easy chairs and tables spread around. People are encouraged to come here just to sit and rest, to chat or read. The church has had a chequered history – dating from the 15th century, it contains some Victorian glass and was extensively repaired in 1913 before being made redundant in 1973.

Just around the corner is St John Timberhill. This is an Anglo-Catholic Church and may date, in part from 1065, although there has been much rebuilding and redesigning, both inside and out, since then. The name comes partly from the timber market which used to take place nearby.

Far left: The railings of St Stephens Church feature coloured orbs representing jewels in his immortal crown

Left: St John's Timberhill in Autumn

Above: In the foreground is the cell in which Julian of Norwich wrote the first book in English by a woman and where she received troubled callers at her window

Above right: The peaceful small garden adjoining the cell

Turn up Ber Street, keeping John Lewis on your right and walk up to Finklegate where the 96 ft tower of St John de Sepulchre, each stage 'stepping back' from the one below, stands elegantly against the skyline. Again, though looking every inch a church built during a single period, it is, in fact, a mixture dating from the fifteenth to the nineteeth centuries. During the Reformation it was stripped of stained glass and the coloured wall pictures covered with white paint. All was reversed in the 19th century and today it is very pretty. It stands on Ber Ridge and is quite a site to visitors as their train pulls in at the railway station down below. I am sure some have wondered if this majestic sight set against the sky is, in fact, the Anglican Cathedral.

Turning back along the road, right into Thorn Lane and right again into Rouen Road, you will soon come to St Julian's Alley on your left. This leads to, arguably, the most famous small church in the city – St Julian's Church. A small attached cell, which can be visited today, was, for twenty years, home to Julian of Norwich (1342–1429). God spoke to her and said 'All shall be well'. She believed that there is no anger, hatred or revenge in God's love. The first woman to write a book in English, her *Revelations of Divine Love* was inspired by her visions, most of them in 1383, and is still in print today. As she became famous, people with troubles would come to her window and talk to her. Julian would then go from her cell into the church and pray: returning, she would tell her guest what God had advised. There is a lovely small garden around the cell, not generally visited.

Leaving the church walk downhill and turn left into King Street. You will soon see St Peter Parmentergate on the left. Standing on a hill with a lovely crenelated tower, the church dates originally from the 11th century, although it was completely rebuilt in the 1500s. It was once very busy as King Street was the most important business street in the city at one time. Like St John de Sepulchre, it suffered during the Reformation when all stained glass and assorted 'frippery', as it was then seen, was removed: again, both churches were returned to

their former glory in the Victorian period. Regrettably, it was declared surplus to requirements in 1981 and interior fittings were removed. It has been used for several purposes since that time, including an advice centre and refuge for prostitutes and a martial arts academy.

Inside is a monument which alone makes a trip worthwhile – the monument to Elizabeth and Richard Berney, erected by Elizabeth's father in 1623. Of particular interest is a carving of a cherub lying on an hour glass, holding a spade: the hour glass represents the short time we are on this earth and the spade the end of life's labours.

Carry on straight up King Street, pass the crossroads and into Tombland. Just before the Edith Cavell pub turn left up Princes Street. A few yards along will find you looking at a beautiful little church – St George Tombland. It is built partly of flint rubble and partly of brick – a most expensive commodity in days gone by. The font is Purbeck marble and was carved in the 13th century. As you might expect from a church in the centre of town, many important citizens worshipped here, as their monuments bear witness. At the west end is a tablet to John Symonds announcing a gift of two shillings a week to the poor 'to continue for ever'. Underneath is a table, most probably for bread bought with the money. Above his customary seat in the church is the monument to Thomas Anguish, both Sheriff and Mayor of the city. A prosperous grocer, he died in 1617 and his memorial costs the vast sum of £20. Of particular interest is that five of his children depicted are either holding skulls or resting their heads on them – a sign that they pre-deceased him.

Head back into Tombland and turn left. Follow the road past Fye Bridge and turn left into Colegate. On the corner is St Clement Colegate, probably the first church to be built north of the river, in about 1040. Just inside the door is a floor slab to the memory of Edward Wood, who was Mayor in the middle of the 17th century and lived in the magnificent house

The monument in St George Tombland to John Symonds who left two shillings a week 'for ever' to buy bread for the poor: the shelf was possibly where the bread was laid out

A quite exceptional monument to the memory of Thomas Anguish above his customary seat in St George Tombland. See text for the reason that five of his children are either holding or esting their heads on skulls

Rare 15th century Flemish glass in St George Tombland

Looking past St George Tombland

The Church of St Clement – the oldest north of the river?

Sundial on the front of The Old Meeting House – if the sun is out, you can check your watch

opposite, now the King of Hearts arts centre and café. His son, Robert, also became Mayor and welcomed Queen Elizabeth I on her visit to the city. Just before departing, in part as a 'thank-you' for some magnificent feasting, she decided to knight him and proceeded on her way. The late 19th century saw a change of emphasis for the church as the area declined in status and the poor needed help.

Follow the alley on your right leading from Colegate to The Old Meeting House, the present home of The Progressive Jewish Community of East Anglia. It has a long history of Dissent, starting life as a Congregationalist church just after the English Civil war with John Cromwell, a relative of the 'Lord Protector' himself, as an early minister. It was designed by that celebrated son of Norwich, Sir Thomas Ivory.

The restored clock of the Church of St Clement on the corner of Colegate

The same architect designed the Octagon Chapel, just up the road. It is a highly original building, octagonal in shape with, inside, eight elegant columns supporting a domed roof. This was, in 1756 when it was built, a very affluent area and so the cost was met by the Unitarian congregation. John Wesley considered it to be too beautiful: critics called it 'the Devil's cucumber frame'. It is an absolute must-see, inside and out.

Walk up Colegate until you come to St George Colegate, built between 1460 and 1513. It is a fine church that was the place of worship of many city traders, particularly wealthy cloth merchants. The pews of rich oak, simple but elegant Reredos, and classical features

The Octagon Chapel: exceedingly lovely or 'The Devil's cucumber frame'?

bear witness to this fact. The inside of the church is a treasure-trove of memorials and epitaphs, including one to William and Alicia Norwich, responsible for the construction of the Nave. Many, however, are fascinating precisely because they refer to real but unremembered lives. Particularly striking and mysterious is the story on a well-worn monument set in the nave floor. It concerns the death of Bryant Lewis, and reads:

'Here lyeth ye body of Mr Bryant Lewis
Who was barbarously murdered
On ye heath near Thetford Sept 13th 1698.
Fifteen wounds this stone veils from thine eyes
But reader hark! Their voice doth pierce the skies.
Vengeance cried Abel's blood gainst cursed Cain,
But better things spake Christ when he was slain.
Both, both cries Lewis gainst his barbarous foe
Blood Lord for Blood, but save his soul from woe.
'Thou shalt do no murder' – Exd XX 13.'

The church will always famously be known as the final resting place of John Crome, buried in the south aisle. There is also a wall tablet, in white marble, to his memory. He was the most eminent of the so-called Norwich School of Artists and details of his life and work are given earlier in the book.

The recently restored tower of St George Colegate

This floor tablet in St George Colegate commemorates the bloody end of Bryant Lewis who was murdered on Thetford Heath in 1698: see text for inscription

Fine white marble memorial to John Crome in St George Colegate; John Crome used to live nearby and drank most evenings in a pub, now gone, a few hundred yards from the place where he worshipped

Turning right as you leave, continue up Colegate and over the busy road ahead where, on the corner with Oak Street, stands St Michael – sometimes referred to as St Miles – Coslany. The chapel facing the road was built by Robert Thorpe in 1500 and experts will tell you that here is as magnificent a piece of flint flushwork as can be found anywhere in England. Once very rich, the church is now used as a hands-on science centre. It is one of five churches in Norwich where bells are still rung – it has eight. Robert Thorpe and his three wives are buried here and, fittingly perhaps, the grandest monument by far in the church attests to his virtue, learning – ie books stacked around him – and certainty of paradise in the form of a cherub about to place on his head the crown of eternal life.

The walk now retraces steps for a few hundred yards and proceeds past the former Norvic shoe factory and carries on up Merchants Street. A previous walk reached the Norwich Technical Institute just past Sir John Soanes' bridge, but then turned back. This time you carry straight on and come to something truly exceptional.

Experts will tell you that here is as fine an example of squared and knapped flint as you will ever find – the Church of St Miles, Coslany, now a 'hands-on' museum

St Andrew and Blackfriars, known simply as the Halls, is a complete medieval monastic complex, and there is nothing like it in the rest of the UK. It was built between 1307 and 1470 by the Dominican Friars. After the Dissolution of the Monasteries, Norwich petitioned King Henry VIII to sell the buildings to the city. Subsequently, the halls were used for feasting, fairs, as a school, a granary and even workhouse. Beautiful outside, with flint elegantly faced with intricate stonework, the most impressive part of the complex is nevertheless the vast and gorgeous St Andrew's Hall with an impressive roof supported by hammer beams. This must be one of the finest concert venues in the kingdom as the acoustics were very important to the early friars and they are excellent. As you sit waiting for the concert to begin, you can survey the over-lifesized gilded portraits of former mayors and sheriffs that line the walls. A modern literary allusion would be to JK Rowling and the Great Hall at Hogwarts – now, did that portrait wink at me or was it an illusion?

The oldest part of the complex is the crypt, now a café and dates from about 1250. It has been suggested that this might have been the sleeping quarters for the 60 friars – the same number, incidentally, as lived and worshipped in the Anglican Cathedral. The cloisters hold weekly antique markets.

Across the street is the largest church in the city after St Peter Mancroft – St Andrew. Built

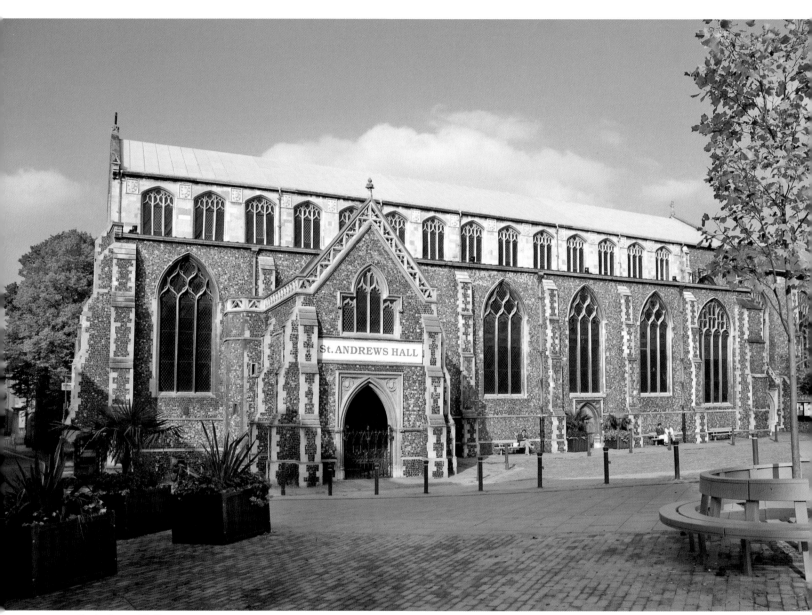

St Andrews Hall
(Daniel Tink - www.scenicnorfolk.co.uk)

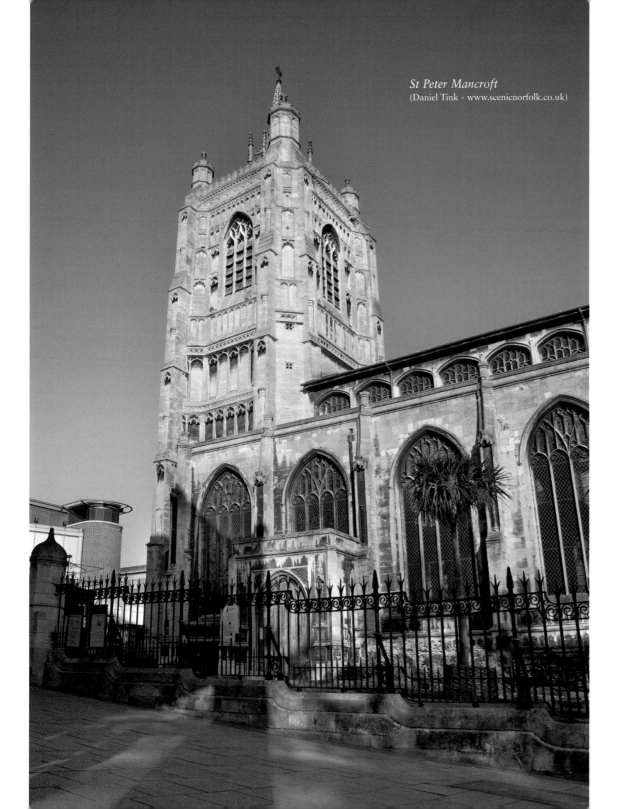

St Peter Mancroft
(Daniel Tink - www.scenicnorfolk.co.uk)

Details of sculpture on the side of St Andrews Church

in what is termed Perpendicular Gothic style in the years following 1478, it verily dominates the skyline as if competing with the splendour of the adjacent Halls – which was quite possibly the intention. For this was a rich church, on a main highway through the city and it contains probably more memorials and epitaphs than any other. Some of Nelson's ancestors are buried here. Amongst others is a very grand one, in brown marble topped with angelic musicians, commemorating Sir John Suckling who held high office under James I. Another wall plaque celebrates the life of Dr Thomas Crowe who died on 10 August 1751, commenting that 'His skill and integrity were revered by all who knew him'. Another informs us of the zeal, diligence, piety and benevolence of the guileless Christian, Samuel Stone, who died in 1848.

Turn left down St Andrews Street when leaving and left again into St John Maddermarket at the top of which stands a church of the same name. An interesting feature here is the 'raised' burial ground which you pass on your right before reaching the church. There were many complaints in the 16th and 17th centuries that such grounds had too many bodies piled up inside them and not enough earth to cover them. The church is quite small but has a fine collection of brasses. It is also, being near to the palace of the Dukes of Norfolk and in the very centre of town, the possessor of many varied graves, plaques and monuments similar to those already mentioned in the Church of St Andrew. One worthy of note is 'the virtuous Lady Margaret', wife of the Thomas Howard, 4th Duke of Norfolk, who died shortly after the birth of her second son and is buried on the north side of the Chancel.

Take a route along Pottergate and cut left up Upper Goat Lane until the road crosses Giles Street where you take a right turn. A little way along you will see the 120 foot high tower of St Giles on the Hill – it used to have a fire basket to guide the ships on the River Wensum below as it stands on the highest ground in the city. The parish of St Giles is mentioned in the Domesday Book (1086) but the present church dates from about 1430. A very early

The Church of St Gregory early on a sunny morning

example of the perpendicular style, it has a peal of eight bells. The remains of Sir Thomas Churchman, Mayor in 1761, lie here. He was a most generous man, giving much of his money to charity, and not shy – his monument lists his greatest donations.

From here, you can walk up Bethel Street and back to St Peter Mancroft where this walk began.

A pleasing jumble: the Belgian Monk pub and the Church of St John Maddermarket

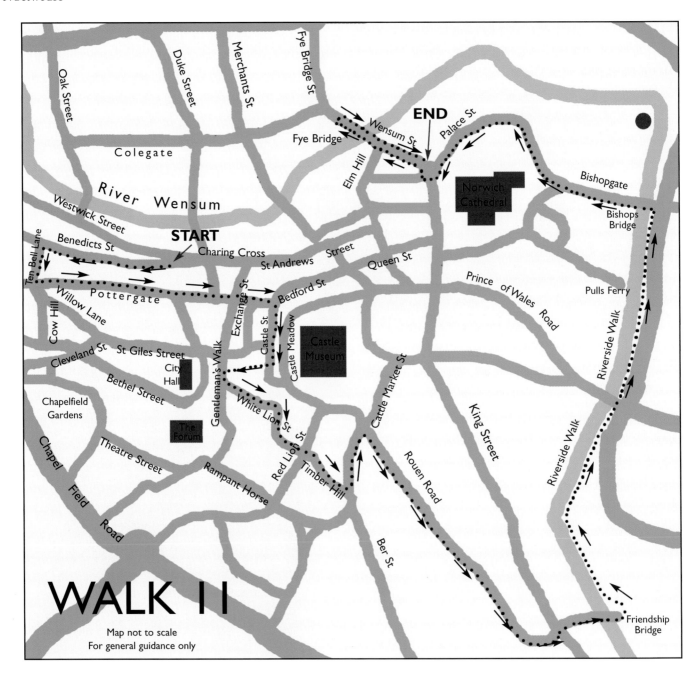

START

END

WALK 11

Map not to scale
For general guidance only

Walk 11

A walk around 27 interesting pubs

Brewing has been linked to Norwich for many hundreds of years. There have always been a lot of pubs – in the 1850s over 600 and even in the 1980s about 200 remained. A visit to City Hall Licensing Department in October 2008 revealed that the city currently had 231 licensed premises – this would include hotels, licensed restaurants, and clubs as well as pubs.

In days gone by, there were probably more unregulated drinking venues than official public houses. Areas of the city such as Coslany were notorious in this respect: any householder who could afford a barrel of ale could sell it from the front room. It may not have been legal but it was impossible to stamp out. Reports on applications from official pubs seeking a renewal of their license last century can be seen on request from the reserve section of the Millennium Library and reveal, time and again, the extent of the problem, one which persisted well into the 20th century. A typical entry for 1911 would say that Inspector so-and-so opposed the renewal of the license of a pub in Oak Street on account of the fact that there were a dozen other drinking establishments within 200 yards and that, these, furthermore, catered to the 'lowest' type of customer. The records also reveal the extent of drinking illegally after hours, and this even at a time when pubs could open at 4am and carry on until 11pm. The fines meted out were quite hefty and legal pubs must have felt very hard done by as they said goodbye to their customers at closing time, only to see them transfer their business, sometimes literally, next door.

Pubs in the city centre would try to retain their customers with some type of speciality entertainment. Cock-fighting was hugely popular in the 1700s and 1800s. Bare-knuckle boxing bouts invariably drew large crowds. Some put on theatrical productions and many tried to hire the unusual – the giant, the midget, the pig that could count, or the giant snake that, at '3 p.m. sharp' would eat a live cat.

Detail of the Golden Star on Colegate

Beers of all sorts were popular and, of course, locally produced. Porter – a rich dark ale – was a favourite with women and said to be good for the throat. Gin became very popular, especially in the 19th century as it was easy and cheap to produce – hence the term 'gin palace'. Such establishments for the poorer classes sometimes displayed a sign which said 'Drunk for a penny. Dead drunk for twopence. Clean straw for nothing.' Hogarth's famous engraving 'Gin Lane' could have referred just as well to areas of Norwich as it did to London.

It is interesting to look at some of the names given to pubs in Norwich. Here are some lists of name types used in Norwich pubs both now and over the centuries.

Biblical names

Adam and Eve
Angel
St Andrew
St Catherine
St Faith
St Giles
St Paul

People – real and fictional

Albert
Artful Dodger
Belgian Monk
Delaney
Duke of Connaught
Duke of Marlborough
Duke of Norfolk
Duke of Sussex
Duke of Wellington
Duke of York
Earl of Cardigan
Earl of Leicester
Edith Cavell
Frank
General Windham
Jack O'Newbury
Jenny Lind
John Bull
Kett
Lord Raglan
Marquis of Granby
Micawber
Mike
Nelson
Prince of Denmark
Prince of Wales
Princess of Wales
Prince Regent
Queen Adelaide
Queen Victoria
Queen of Hungary
Queen of Iceni
Seamus O'Rourke
Shakespeare
Sir Garnet Wolseley
Crome
William IV

Professions and trade names

Baker
Bank
Boatswain
Bricklayer
Cabinet Maker
Chandlers
Coachmaker
Coldstream Guard
Cooper
Distillery
Eastern Union Railway
Fishmonger
Foundry
Grocer
Hot Presser
Ironmonger
Lawyer
Brewer – usually 'Jolly'
Butcher – usually 'Jolly'
Dyer – usually 'Jolly'
Farmer – usually 'Jolly'
Hatter – usually 'Jolly'
Malster – usually 'Jolly'
Mariner – usually 'Jolly'
Rifleman
Trowel and Hammer
Waterman
Wig and Pen
Woolkpack
Yarn
Yarn Factory

Food
Artichoke
Blueberries
Grapes

Mustard Pot
Pineapple
Rosemary and Thyme
Ribs of Beef
Shoulder of Mutton
(Slug and) Lettuce

Animals and insects

Arabian Horse
Bee Hive
Bird-in-hand
Black eagle
Black/White/Grey Horse
Boar's Head
Bull
Cat (and Fiddle)
Cock
Crocodile
Dolphin
(Dun) Cow
Elephant
Fox and Hounds
Golden Dog
Golden Lion
Goose (and Gridiron)
Green Dragon
Griffin
Hampshire Hog
Lamb
(Lame) Dog
Nag
Nightingale
Ostrich
Parrot
Peacock
Pig

Pigeon
Rat
Raven
Red Lion
Reindeer
Slug
Swan
Turkey
Unicorn
White Hart

Places

Angel Pleasure Gardens
Bank Plain
Ber Street Gates
Bishop's Bridge
Castle
City
Colchester
Denmark
Derby
Duke's Palace
Essex
Ipswich
London
Fye Bridge
Norfolk
Norwich
Orford
Oxford
Sandringham
Somerset
Suffolk
Tombland
Yarmouth

Plants and Trees
Blue Bell
Cherry Tree
Elm
Rose/Red Rose/White Rose
Walnut Tree
Vine

Sports

Boxer
(Compleat) Angler
Cricketer

Miscellaneous

Balloon

Bell
Bell Vue
Black Chequers
Birdcage
Catherine Wheel
Causeway
Comfortably Numb
East End Retreat
Eaton Cottage
Eight Ringers
Evening Gun
Flower Pot
Free Trade
Golden Can
Great Eastern Vaults
Ha Ha
Hope
Indulge
Jumpin' Jack

Lock and Key
Maids Head
Mischief
Murderer
Norwegian Blue
Nursery
Old Friends
Orgasmic
Rainbow
Refreshers
Spear-in-hand
Ten Bells
Thorn
Trafalgar
True Comrades
Volunteer
Waterloo
York
ZiZi

Perhaps you could at one time hear the chimes of ten church bells from here

This walk begins at the top of St Lawrence Steps, where walk four ended and walk five began. To your left as you leave the steps is Comfortably Numb, a state-of-the-art Sports Bar, with a large flat-screen TV. It is quite small but popular with locals who like to watch the main sporting events from satellite TV. WiFi is here. Live Bands perform on Thursdays. There is a disabled-friendly toilet.

Cross the road and proceed back down St Benedicts Street. A few hundred yards down you will come to an old pub called The Ten Bells. There is some dispute as to how it came by its name but it seems likely that it was from here that you could hear the peal of ten church bells. The pub dates from at least 1745 and it has a homely and comfortable air about it. A quiet pub, it features hand-pumped Greene King IPA and Greene King Old Speckled Hen. It is easily accessible to the disabled.

Traditional in character – The Plough in St Benedicts Street

The area around Delaneys and The Halls has recently undergone substantial renovation with new paving, street furniture and seating. It is popular on sunny lunchtimes with office workers and others out for an al fresco lunch

'The Halls' host many special events, not all of them ecclesiastical in nature

Mike's Bar in Bedford Street

St Swithins Alley is opposite and it was reputedly down here that the Hampshire Hog existed in the 19th century, famous as the tenant was John 'Licker' Pratt, the champion bare-knuckle prize fighter. Here you could play a game called 'Logats', which has died out now, but was once very popular. It consisted of laying down a jack and then throwing three club-like 'logats' at it – the winner was the player whose logat landed nearest the jack.

Just along the road is The Plough which has an intricate exterior. Inside it is also a place that makes drinkers want to linger. There is a large garden at the rear.

Turn left up Ten Bell Lane and left again into Pottergate. Ahead of you is Micawber's Tavern, celebrating Dickens' famous character who was always fighting off tradesmen demanding payment but who ended up triumphant in the New World. He is a celebration of hope in the face of adversity and, in this traditional venue, can be imagined taking life very easy indeed and trying to get another pint of hand-drawn beer on credit. These currently include ales such as Nelson's Revenge and Elgoods Cambridge.

Walk along Pottergate, past The Birdcage on your left – a no-nonsense boozer on two floors where Greene King IPA and Abbot are served – and you will come to The Belgian Monk. This striking gabled venue is very popular, especially for those who like Belgian bottled beer. Care is needed, however, as the Belgian can be much more potent than the English beer of the bottled variety and it is easy to get up to leave only to find that your legs don't work anymore. Good food at reasonable rates is available, too.

The great working man's leader, Keir Hardie, is commemorated by this club in the Lanes

Just ahead, on the corner of St John Maddermarket and Lobster Lane is Mike's Bar, previously Boltz. This is a cosy, modern bar which, at time of writing, offers jacket potatoes and 'world famous chilli', along with draught and bottled beers.

Continue into Bedford Street and past Frank's Bar on the left, which, a short while ago, was a sandwich bar and café. Disabled access is good and regular beers include Adnam's Bitter and Green King. It is a sign of the times that, while larger pubs are going out of business due to both cheap alcohol being available in the supermarkets and the smoking ban, smaller establishments like Frank's Bar and Mike's Bar, are opening up. Maybe this more personal approach is the future as opposed to the huge themed pubs that thrived in the nineties.

The alley alongside Frank's Bar leads to Bedfords, popular with the younger crowd. There is a bar upstairs and one in the crypt. Meals are served lunchtime and evenings.

At the top of the street, opposite the NatWest Bank, is The Wild Man. This traditional pub commemorates, not, as some believe, a resident of Bethel Street 'lunaticks' Home but Peter, supposedly suckled by a she-bear in the Forest of Herenhausen. Legend has it that George I came across him whilst hunting and brought him back to England. Attempts to educate him

Tucked away - Bedfords

A fascinating story – the Wild Man – see text

failed and he escaped, turning up in Norwich. As he could not speak and was destitute, he was incarcerated in Bridewell prison until reclaimed by a Thomas Fenns to whom George I had entrusted his welfare. He went on to live to the age of 73 and when he died, in 1785, he was a celebrity. It is not hard to imagine that he would have been a most attractive business proposition in these times as many pubs gained a profit from putting on what were, in effect, freak shows and perhaps this is how he earned his living.

Turning right, proceed down London Street and first left past Waterstone's (previously Ottaker's) fine bookshop. On your left, down a small alley, is The Walnut Tree Shades. In his entertaining book of 1975,'The Inns and Taverns of Old Norwich', Dr John Young recounts how, with its budgeriagar and collection of buffalo horns, this was then a centre for singing and conviviality. It has changed a little as, apart from attracting city workers for a 'quick one' on the way home, it now it plays hosts to local bands on Thursdays and weekend nights can get very crowded. It is still friendly, and notable for appealing to people from all walks of life and of all ages. Disabled people can gain easy access. There is a restaurant upstairs.

Leaving The Walnut Tree Shades, turn left and you will come out in Gentleman's Walk. Just ahead, to your left, is one of the most photographed pubs in town, the Sir Garnet Wolseley. This five storied, bulbous and balconied structure offers some fine views of the market place if you wish to take your drink upstairs. It is the only pub in the Market proper – there is Refreshers just off the main drag, top right – and it is a good place to view the hustle and

The Sir Garnet Wolseley
(Daniel Tink - www.scenicnorfolk.co.uk)

bustle of the Market. Sir Garnet is famous for arriving too late to save General Gordon at Khartoum. This was entirely due, however, to the procrastination of Gladstone's administration at home, and comprehensive victory over Arabi Pasha ensued. Sir Garnet Wolseley became a national hero in 1882. Prior to its inauguration as a pub, it was a butcher's shop. In 1858 was displayed the Great Ox, a mammoth beast by all accounts, soon to be roasted on Lakenham Cricket Ground in a celebrated Norwich holiday event. Featured beers include hand-pumped Adnam's Broadside and Greene King IPA.

Carry on along Gentleman's Walk and take a left at White Lion Street, in the middle of which you will find Henry's. This was previously The Lamb and has an exceedingly chequered history. As an example, the landlord, John Aggas, a reportedly kind-hearted man, was murdered in 1787 by his brother-in-law, Timothy Hardy. By all accounts, the murderer was jealous of the success of his relation in maintaining such a fine ale house. One night in November, drunk with his friends at the nearby Magpie public house, he decided to invade The Lamb, have a great free party and then smash the place to pieces. Using his key, he and his friends entered the Lamb and made merry. John Aggas, interrupted in his sleep, tried to defend his property. Timothy Hardy had just decided to turn on all the taps in order to waste the beer when John Aggas interrupted him. Hardy stabbed John Aggar in the stomach. Timothy Hardy was hanged from the gallows in front of the adjacent Norwich Castle but not before suffering the most terrible torment in his mind. His cries into the night for forgiveness were to no avail.

You will see the Bell Hotel at the end of this street. Along with The Maids Head this is one of the two surviving ancient hotels of Norwich. It is known for hosting the Revolution Club, which caused the government some anxiety although it appears to have done little more than chant the maxims of the French Revolution to little effect. More dangerous was the

Far left: The Lamb – scene of a terrible late night party in 1787

Left: One of two great surviving coaching inns – The Bell Hotel – the other is The Maids Head

*Hereby hangs a gruesome tale –
The Gardeners/The Murderers
pub*

infamous 'Hell Fire Club' which professed itself inimicable to government and anti-Methodist. After an evening's heavy drinking the 'gentlemen' would try to find something to attack, preferably a Methodist, and, in 1754, one Minister suffered serious injury. All sorts of other, genuinely political, debating clubs also met here in the 19th century. WiFi access is available. Tasting notes are provided for the ever-changing guest ales. Both the extensive food selection and ales served are at reasonable prices.

For lovers of modern theatre, The Bell holds a special place as the 'retreat' for Arnold Wesker following a string of rejection slips from London publishers and theatre proprietors. He took refuge in the kitchens as a cook writing at night and he gradually regained his confidence. A brilliant series of plays eventually catapulted him to fame as one of the 'angry young men' of the 1950s alongside Joe Orton. One, 'The Kitchen' (1957) directly refers to his routine at breakfast-time here preparing porridge bacon, eggs and kippers for the hotel's guests.

The view from the riverbank is very different now. Today, you will see mainly pleasure craft as you sip your drink in a riverside pub, but this fine Wherry, the Norfolk Hero, *built in 1860 and used to transport chimney pots, is typical of the vessels plying their trade on the water in the 19th century*

A few doors away is a pub, originally called the Gardeners' Arms but also known as the Murderers, and the sign at present has both names on the opposite sides. This area was quite rough and, one evening, a prostitute failed to get her payment from a client. An argument ensued and the prostitute was knifed to death. This is a multi-floor pub, much bigger than it appears from the outside, and serves real ale. It is very popular with city workers and a younger crowd. It has WiFi access and satellite TV.

Walk up Timberhill, left into Golden Ball Street and right into Rouen Road. At the bottom, where this road meets King Street, you will see the clean white lines of the Friendship Bridge which will take you over the river. Turn left and walk along the river, probably dotted with fishermen, towards the Anglican Cathedral towering in the distance. You will come to an open space on your right around which is the new Riverside entertainment complex – a multiplex cinema, restaurants, a health club and nightclubs. There are also two large pubs facing the river – the Queen of Iceni and Norwegian Blue (this has a toilet accessible for disabled people and is a very quiet and pleasant place to linger and look at the boats passing by), both having large seating area outside. At weekends, this part of town is frenetic with club and pub goers as this area forms an 'L' shape with the other main clubbing area, Prince of Wales Road. In the week, however, it is quite the opposite and is a good place to meet for a pub lunch or supper. Traditional English food is favoured such as fish and chips, bangers and mash or gammon steak, egg and chips.

Walking straight on at the cross roads, note the Compleat Angler on your right, a traditional pub popular with drinkers who want to sit and watch activity on the river. It boasts WiFi access, a function room and serves London Pride, Green King and Fullers ales amongst others.

Carry on until you come to Bishop's Bridge, referred to on Walk 1. Almost opposite is the 17th century Bridge House pub, situated on the site of Lollards Pit with a plaque on the wall to commemorate the burning of many unfortunate souls.

Across the river is the Red Lion, a most attractive pub which serves hand-pumped ales such as Adnams Bitter, Shepherd Neame Spitfire and Woodforde's Wherry . You can sit by the river and access WiFi here. There is a large car park adjacent. Sunday lunchtime features a carvery.

Carry on up Bishopsgate which bends to the right at the top and soon, on your right, you will see arguably Norwich's most famous and venerable pub – the Adam and Eve. Inside, there are more steps up and down than you can shake a stick at, leading to or from small snug rooms containing high-back settles. Nobody knows exactly when it was built but it dates from at least the 13th century when both it and the Red Lion just mentioned were the property of the monks of the Great Hospital. George Borrow drank here often. It is reputed

Far left: The Queen of Iceni in the new Riverside Quarter

Left: An ideal spot to watch the world – and boats – go by: the Compleat Angler beside Foundry Bridge

to be haunted with a number of monk-like ghosts as well as that of Lord Sheffield who perished close by during Kett's rebellion. A selection of real ales is available.

Leave the Adam and Eve by walking up Palace Street. On your left will be found a pretty pub with an outside seating area, called the Wig and Pen. This is very popular with city professionals for lunches. It won the 'Le Routier Food Pub of the Year, East Anglia 2005/6' award, and serves hand-pumped ales including Buffy's Norwich Terrier and Fullers London Pride. Major sporting events are shown on widescreen TVs and disabled people will not find access a problem.

You soon arrive at the junction of Tombland, with the Maids Head Hotel on your right. For the moment, though, just note the location of this ancient inn, cross the road and turn right. The street ahead of you is worth a slight detour as it contains some very interesting pubs in a short stretch of road. To begin with, you are now standing in front of Take 5 which appeals to people who do not necessarily feel at home in pub-like atmospheres: it is a café and art gallery as well as an ale house, and also serves excellent food. Walk down past the entrance to Elm Hill and you will see a smart pub, The Lawyers, which is popular with professionals and serves Thai food. Opposite is the huge Glasshouse, well known for an ever-changing selection of guest ales at low prices and typical pub-grub. A few yards takes you to the river and the Ribs of Beef: this was most likely its speciality food in days gone by. Today it is a friendly pub with a loyal clientele, is WiFi linked, and features hand-pumped ales including Elgood's Black Dog and Woodforde's Wherry. Immediately across the bridge is the Mischief, especially popular with a younger crowd and those who like to watch sporting events live on flat-screen television. Double back again to the Maids Head Hotel, a couple of hundred yards up the road on your left. This is a good place to end the walk, at possibly the oldest inn in England, although it does not look like it from the outside with its lower elevations of brick and Tudor-style timbered top.

We know that, in 1287, it was a hospice for monks attached to the Bishop's Palace. The Black Prince, Cardinal Wolsey, Queen Catherine and even Good Queen Bess herself are said to have stayed here. There is a bedroom named after Queen Elizabeth I but, on the other hand, so there is in many other hotels the length and breadth of the land. We know she came here on one of the many travels around her kingdom, but by all accounts she feasted and travelled on before dusk. She also visited the palace of the Earl of Surrey near Mousehold Heath, but surely she would have stayed there? The original parlour bar is much like it always has been and there is an atmosphere about the hotel that makes it a wrench to leave. We have more than one account by citizens - including Mayor Anguish in 1611, featured in Walk 1 – who thought the same and suffered marital discord as a result. There is 800 years of history in every corridor and room: if you only take one drink on this walk, there is no more appropriate or enjoyable spot for it than this.

Below left: A popular stop while walking along the river – The Red Lion

Below right: A legendary Norwich pub – The Adam and Eve

Popular with professionals for lunch, and for good food generally – the Wig and Pen

Very large and popular with an ever-changing selection of ales and good food – The Glasshouse in Wensum Street

The Ribs of Beef and Fye Bridge

The Maids Head Hotel – Elizabeth I slept here; or maybe she didn't

20 Questions

How well do you know Norwich? Here is a family quiz to find out. The answers can all be found in the book.

1. **The Norwich football team is known as?**

    a)   The Lions
    b)   The Green and Yellows
    c)   The Canaries
    d)   The Conquerors

2.   **Norwich Anglican Cathedral was started by?**

    a)   King Henry VIII
    b)   The 10th Duke of Norfolk
    c)   The Pope
    d)   Herbert de Losinga

3. **The University of East Anglia was begun in?**

    a)   1735
    b)   Medieval times
    c)   1980
    d)   The 1960s

4. **In October 2008, the number of licensed premises in Norwich was?**

    a)   453
    b)   About the same as 200 years ago
    c)   231
    d)   Thousands

5. **The present slogan for the city is?**

    a)   Norwich – a fine city
    b)   Norwich – it's got everything
    c)   Come shop: come drop: come to Norwich
    d)   Norwich: the finest city in the Kingdom

6.   Julian of Norwich is famous for?

a)   Being the first female to write a book in English
b)   Standing up for Anglicans against Edward I
c)   Defending Norwich against French invaders
d)   Living to be 112 years old

7.   Which of the following industrial enterprises are NOT associated with the city?

a)   Caley's chocolate
b)   Boulton & Paul
c)   Wills cigarettes
d)   Colman's mustard

8.   Who is often referred to as 'the First Lady of Norwich'?

a)   Margaret Thatcher
b)   Delia Smith
c)   St Agatha
d)   Madonna

9.   The original use of the Assembly House was as a?

a)   Centre for the entertainment of the gentry
b)   Conference venue
c)   Prison
d)   Art gallery

10.   Who finally defeated Robert Kett on Mousehold Heath in 1549?

a)   Queen Elizabeth I
b)   The Marquis of Northampton
c)   No-one: he won the day
d)   The Earl of Warwick

11.   The Bethel Hospital, built in the late 17th Century, was for?

a)   Curable lunatics
b)   Soldiers who had lost a limb in Empire Wars
c)   Lepers
d)   Children's ailments

12. Norwich Union, now Aviva Worldwide, has its Norwich headquarters in?

    a) Norfolk Street
    b) Norwich Parade
    c) Surrey Street
    d) Essex Road

13. Norwich Castle was begun in?

    a) 687 AD
    b) About 1200 BC
    c) Probably 1067 AD
    d) Probably the late 1400s AD

14. How did a major credit card company rate Norwich shopping, as regards customer satisfaction, in 2006?

    a) Absolutely hopeless
    b) Number two, behind Bluewater
    c) The best
    d) Good in some ways but must improve

15. Why is Admiral Lord Nelson famous?

    a) He discovered a cure for the Black Death
    b) He was the first man to sail around the world
    c) He won many battles in India, especially the Battle of Mingpur in 1807, which secured colonial domination over that area
    d) He won many famous battles, notably the Battle of Trafalgar in 1805

16. Why is John Crome considered a famous name?

    a) He is perhaps the most famous of the 'Norwich School' of artists
    b) He invented central heating
    c) He published a book about the effect of wealth upon general wellbeing
    d) He invented the 'overarm' delivery of a ball in cricket

17. What is the name of the church opposite the Forum?

a) The Church of St Edmund the Confessor
b) St Gregorys
c) The Church of St John the Baptist
d) St Peter Mancroft

18. **Which hotel is the oldest in the city?**

a) The Nelson
b) Premier Inn
c) The Maids Head
d) Travelodge

19. **Which ONE of the following statements is incorrect?**

a) At one time, Norwich was reputed to have more churches that London
b) Coslany has always been a fairly affluent part of the city
c) Brewing and chocolate making were two of the city's main industries in the 19th century
d) Oak Street had bad reputation for 'unofficial' pubs well into the 20th century

20. **Which ONE of the following statements is correct?**

a) The Adam and Eve pub is about 300 years old
b) In the 2nd World War Lord Haw Haw predicted the destruction of the 1938 City Hall by German bombers
c) Happily, all redundant Norwich churches have found alternative uses
d) The Black Death killed over half of the city's population

Quiz Answers

1 c	11 a
2 d	12 c
3 d	13 c
4 c	14 c
5 a	15 d
6 a	16 a
7 c	17 d
8 b	18 c
9 a	19 b
10 d	20 b

Postscript

Create your own walk.

The author and Halsgrove hope you have enjoyed this journey through a great city. For the young ones and young at heart, here is a final idea: create your own tour using the following famous people, places and enterprises as a guide. All are featured in these pages as are the maps with which to find them. Link the walk up as you see fit!

1. Admiral Lord Nelson
2. Edith Cavell
3. Jeremiah Coleman
4. Delia Smith
5. Boulton & Paul
6. Robert Kett
7. St Benedict
8. The Victorian Plantation Garden
9. Mousehold Heath
10. Sir Denys Lasdun
11. George Borrow
12. Caley's chocolate
13. Sir Thomas Browne
14. John Crome
15. The Murderer's pub
16. Norwich Union – now Aviva Worldwide
17. Baroness Amos
18. The Ten Bells
19. The Forum
20. Henry, 15th Duke of Norfolk

St Gregory's Green
(Daniel Tink - www.scenicnorfolk.co.uk)